"Cyndy Salzmann and her book *Beyond Groundhogs a...* a party right now, and for every occasion. I learned ... days, activities for different age groups, even questions ... conversations. Plus I found some great decorating ideas and recipes for come-hither foods. Within the pages of *Beyond Groundhogs and Gobblers* you'll find complete party kits. Have a happy one!"

—Lauraine Snelling, author of The Red River of the
North series and *The Way of Women*

"Cyndy is one of those rare instruments of God that can impart great wisdom while delighting those around her with humor and warmth. When Cyndy talks, everybody listens—because she knows God and loves His people!"

—Nancy Cobb, author of *The Politically Incorrect Wife*

"*Beyond Groundhogs and Gobblers* is a superb resource for parents who want to make holidays meaningful and memorable for their children. Salzmann makes celebrating easy as she offers the historical and spiritual significance of each American holiday, then provides activities and recipes for kids of all ages. I wish I had had this book when home-schooling my son."

—Pat J. Sikora, author, speaker and home-schooling parent

Beyond Groundhogs and Gobblers

Putting Meaning Back into Your Holiday Celebrations

Cyndy Salzmann

CHRISTIAN PUBLICATIONS, INC.
CAMP HILL, PENNSYLVANIA

CHRISTIAN PUBLICATIONS, INC.
3825 Hartzdale Drive, Camp Hill, PA 17011
www.christianpublications.com

Faithful, biblical publishing since 1883

Beyond Groundhogs and Gobblers
ISBN: 0-87509-992-0
© 2004 by Cyndy Salzmann
All rights reserved
Printed in the United States of America

05 06 07 08   5 4 3 2

Unless otherwise indicated,
Scripture is taken from the HOLY BIBLE:
NEW INTERNATIONAL VERSION ®.
Copyright © 1973, 1978, 1984 by the
International Bible Society. Used by
permission of Zondervan Bible Publishers.

Scripture labeled "NASB" is taken from
the New American Standard Bible ®,
© 1960, 1962, 1963, 1968, 1971, 1972, 1973,
1975, 1977, 1995 by The Lockman Foundation.
Used by permission.

Scripture labeled "KJV" is taken from
the Holy Bible: King James Version.

Scripture labeled "Amp." is taken from the Amplified Bible.
© 1954, 1958 by The Lockman Foundation, © 1962, 1964, 1965
by Zondervan Publishing House.
All rights reserved.

Dedication

To Becki,
for her assistance, wisdom, enthusiasm,
encouragement and treasured friendship.

And to my very first group of "simple celebrators":
Allison, Becki, Boots, Deb, Floy, Joy, Kim,
Karen, Rosemary and Rhonda.

Thank you, my dear sisters in Christ!

Contents

August

September

October

November

December

Introduction

Have a feast and celebrate. (Luke 15:23)

I'm one of those people who can find *any* excuse to celebrate. In fact, one of my fondest memories of kindergarten was the discovery of Groundhog Day. I remember thinking that any teacher willing to throw a party in honor of a sleepy rodent had to be fun!

As a child, all of the clothes for my Barbie dolls were related to parties. Barbie had a "ski party outfit," a "pajama party set," a satin dress for her "dance party" and, of course, an elaborate wedding gown for the biggest party of her life. I spent hours, either alone or with my best friend Janie, planning all the details of Barbie's parties, from food to decorations. We'd then retreat to the kitchen to whip up a box of Chef Boyardee pizza for our own—what else?—pizza party!

Although he'll never admit it, I think one of the reasons my husband was attracted to me was my zeal for celebration. On one of our early dates, I greeted John from my front porch dressed in red, white and blue and waving the American flag. When he asked what all the fuss was about, I exuberantly replied, "It's Flag Day!" Once inside, he saw that my roommates and I had strung white lights throughout the living room and kitchen and had prepared a dinner with all red, white or blue food. The little skewers of raspberries, blueberries and mini-marshmallows may not have been a gourmet delight, but they were definitely fun!

Today, my family's love for celebration continues to be a bit "over the top." In addition to the traditional holidays, we celebrate when someone has a great day *and* when someone has a bad day. We celebrate the day before a family member leaves on a trip and, of course, when he or she returns. We even build a party each fall weekend around University of Nebraska football games (and none of us even attended the university). If someone comes up with even the slightest excuse to celebrate, we're there!

Having fun is great, and I think that God delights in our celebrations—big and small. However, through the years, He has taught me that His reason for commanding us to celebrate special days is much deeper than just having fun. Holidays give us an opportunity to pause in the midst of a chaotic world and take note of what's truly important: God's deep love for His people, His character, His provision, His sacrifice, His mercy, His grace and His gifts. This is why these special days are called holidays—literally "holy days"—so that we can take time to worship the One who made each and every day.

This realization has given me a new attitude. Of course, I still want to have fun, but I don't want to miss what God has to teach me (and my children) in the midst of the celebration.

The search for meaning in the revelry prompted me to do some digging before I began planning our next Flag Day dinner. I wanted to find out *why* we celebrate this holiday in America—and more importantly, what it means to me, as a citizen and as a Christian. My discoveries led me to do the same for Valentine's Day so that as I helped my children decorate their Valentine's Day boxes for school, I could make sure they learned the story of the brave Christian martyr, St. Valentine. And so it went until I had discovered the "holy" behind a number of our favorite holidays.

And, much to my delight, discovering the "holiness" behind the holidays and building our traditions around those truths has transformed our celebrations from just "fun" to positively joyous! And, dear reader, that's the reason I'm writing this book. In fact, I'm practically bursting to share what God has taught me! I know from personal experience that you will never look at a holiday the same way once you take the time to find the "holy" in it. You can use the information, age-appropriate activities and recipes that I have provided to aid you in instilling the importance of these holy days in the lives of your children. The Table Talk questions and discussion topics that you'll find in each chapter are there to help you get conversations started about the significance of holidays.

If the thought of the annual Labor Day picnic in your backyard or your turn to host Thanksgiving dinner has you up late at night working on excuses, this book is for you. Or, if you look forward to holidays but end up so exhausted with preparations that you can't enjoy yourself, read on. Or, if you are like me and are looking for any excuse to celebrate, trust me—you are going to have so much fun reading this book! Regardless of your reason for picking up this book, my prayer is that you will be equipped to pass to future generations the "holiness" of our holidays. In turn, you will find true joy (and hopefully some fun) just around the corner!

Why Celebrate?

Celebrate your festivals. (Nahum 1:15)

My husband, John, and I had a rather interesting conversation recently about a book called *Skipping Christmas* by John Grisham. The story focuses on a couple of empty nesters who, fed up with the commercialization of the holiday season, decide to just "skip" Christmas and take a Caribbean cruise. The story describes the resulting chaos and the extremely comical consequences of their decision.

I found myself laughing out loud (even in public places) as I read of the woes of two people bent on "skipping" Christmas—probably because I could see myself in many of the same situations. On the other hand, my husband, definitely the most frugal of our little family unit, couldn't understand what the fuss was all about. He felt the couple had made a perfectly rational decision by boycotting the commercial aspects of the season—an idea that most people would do well to consider.

As you can imagine, it was this last statement that made me extremely nervous. And what made me even more uneasy was the fact that I didn't have a truly convincing response. I realized it was time to find out what God has to say on the subject of holidays, just in case this subject of "skipping" Christmas came up again.

Celebrate to Remember

Celebrate this day as a lasting ordinance for the generations to come. (Exodus 12:17)

One of Webster's definitions of the word *celebrate* is "to mark or take note of."[1] God instructs us to celebrate—to "mark"—certain days each year so we won't forget their importance or fail to pass it on to subsequent generations.

A perfect example of God's desire for us to mark these special days is his explicit instructions for celebrating the Passover, found in the book of Exodus:

> *And when your children ask you, "What does this ceremony mean to you?" then tell them, "It is the Passover sacrifice to the LORD, who passed over the houses of the Israelites in Egypt and spared our homes when he struck down the Egyptians." (12:26-27)*

We need to mark our holidays in such a way that future generations understand why we are celebrating. Unfortunately, in the United States today, we have lost the historic significance of many of our holidays. As a child, I assumed St. Patrick's Day was about good luck and leprechauns. Today, the focus seems to be on how much green beer an individual can consume. (Did you know that St. Patrick's Day, a holy day, now outranks

New Year's Eve in the number of drunken drivers on our roads?[2]) When I found out that St. Patrick was a dedicated missionary who brought the light of Jesus to a people lost in the occult practices of Druidism, I just about cried. How could we have forgotten the significance of this great holiday? Unfortunately, it was pretty easy to forget because no one cared enough to pass the true meaning on.

Celebrate to Honor

"You must observe my Sabbaths. This will be a sign between me and you, for the generations to come, so you may know that I am the LORD, who makes you holy." (31:13)

A *celebrity*, literally a "celebrated person," is well-known for his or her achievements. God wants to hold such a position of honor in the lives of His people. Placing God at the center of our holiday celebrations helps to keep Him in that rightful position. When we fail to recognize the "holy" in our holidays, we fail to honor God.

In some sense, I might know (at least a little bit) how God feels when He is left out of our celebrations. You see, my first child, Freddy, was born the evening before my birthday. And although Freddy's healthy birth certainly ranked at the top of my list of birthday gifts, the celebration of *my* birth has never been the same.

Prior to 1986, the preparations leading up to March 9 focused on me. After Freddy was born, I felt guilty asking for a "fresh" birthday cake when there was half a cake already in the refrigerator. I would also rather spend more of our budget planning a fun party or buying a gift for little Freddy than on myself. After all, I was an adult. Birthdays are for kids. (Can't you just hear the violins playing?) Actually, my husband, John, did his best to make my day special, but the reality was that it was still overshadowed by Freddy's party.

Several years ago, things changed in our household. Armed with basic skills from his junior high cooking class, Freddy surprised me on my birthday with a homemade version of my favorite sour cream chocolate cake with raspberries and whipped cream. He even spent half the day on his birthday to bake it! Of course, in proper motherly "martyr" form I said, "Oh, Freddy, you didn't have to do this!" And he replied, "I know, Mom. But I know how much you like it and I love you. Happy birthday!"

Well, you can guess the rest of the story: I melted into a puddle of tears. I think it's a pretty good bet that God reacts the same way (well, maybe not melting into tears, but I'm sure He's pretty happy) when we forgo our agendas to honor Him on His special days.

Celebrate to Testify

"This day is sacred to the LORD your God. Do not mourn or weep." . . . "Go and enjoy choice food and sweet drinks, and send some to those who have nothing prepared." (Nehemiah 8:9-10)

Holocaust survivor and author Corrie ten Boom once said, "The world does not read the Bible. The world reads you and me."[3] We don't like to think people are watching us, but they are. In fact, they are watching our every move. (Pretty scary, huh?)

In the book of Zechariah, God vows to send a plague to those who do not celebrate the Feast of Tabernacles (see Zechariah 14:17-19). Seem a bit harsh for not celebrating a holiday? What this tells me is that God didn't establish holidays and instruct us to celebrate them just to make Him feel good. Our celebration of God's faithfulness, goodness and protection is a powerful testimony to those around us.

It's interesting to note that in the Gospels we don't see Jesus skipping any holidays. Feast of Dedication? Jesus was there (see John 10:22-23). Feast of Tabernacles? He refused to miss it—even though it was dangerous for Him to attend (see 7:1-10). A family wedding? Are you kidding? This was the site of His first miracle (see 2:1-11). Passover? Not a chance of missing that celebration of God's protection, even as a child (see Luke 2:41-42). Jesus even chose the Passover Seder to symbolize the crux of our faith: His death as payment for sin (see Matthew 26:17-30).

As Christians, we are called to be "salt" (15:13) and "light" (15:14) in a tasteless, dark world. Holidays provide a powerful opportunity to do so.

Celebrate to Build Community

I have been reminded of your sincere faith, which first lived in your grandmother Lois and in your mother Eunice and, I am persuaded, now lives in you also. (2 Timothy 1:5)

Someone once said that "tradition is the living faith of those now dead."[4] We only have a short time before our children are on their own, so establishing holiday traditions is a great way to pass along important truths and family values that they will carry with them into their adult lives.

One of the traditions in our family is to place our Christmas tree next to a picture of Jesus. The placement of the tree next to the picture wasn't intentional the first time we did it. I remember my daughter, Liz, noticing the picture and exclaiming, "This is where our tree belongs!" Since then, every time we look at the Christmas tree, we have a powerful reminder of the true reason for our Christmas celebration.

Remember, a tradition doesn't have to be elaborate to be special. In fact, it's important to choose traditions carefully to avoid allowing the tradition to become more important than the reason for doing it.

For a couple of years, we tried to establish a tradition of attending a sunrise service on Easter morning. This had a special meaning to me as a reminder of celebrating Easter at sunrise on the beach during a missions trip in college. As you can imagine, getting the family up and dressed to attend a sunrise service was quite an ordeal—too much of an ordeal. By the time we dragged ourselves to church we were not in the most "worshipful" moods. We were allowing the "tradition" to interfere with the reason we had established it.

While traditions are a powerful way to pass our faith to future generations, decide together what makes your holiday most meaningful and then include it. Use the holidays as God intended: to connect more intimately with Him and with each other.

Celebrate to Have Fun!

This day is sacred to our Lord. Do not grieve, for the joy of the LORD is your strength. (Nehemiah 8:10)

German philosopher Frederick Nietzsche once commented scornfully regarding Christians, "I would believe in their salvation if they looked a little more like people who had been saved!"[5] He has a good point, doesn't he? Why would an unbelieving world be attracted to a bunch of sullen party poopers?

Second Chronicles 30:21-27 tells about a Passover celebration so full of praise, food, music and encouragement that it went on for seven days. And can you guess what these exuberant Israelites decided to do at the end of the seven days? They decided to keep celebrating for another week!

There was great joy in Jerusalem. . . . The priests . . . stood to bless the people, and God heard them, for their prayer reached heaven. (2 Chronicles 30:26-27)

That's my kind of celebration!

Andrew Murray says, "Joy is not a luxury or mere accessory in the Christian life. It is a sign that we are really living in God's wonderful love, and that love satisfies."[6] As the Sunday school song says, "If you're happy and you know it, then your face will surely show it!" So clap your hands, stomp your feet, shout "Amen!" and most of all, smile!

"The religion that makes a man look sick certainly won't cure the world."

—Phillip Brooks[7]

Notes

1. "Celebrate," *Merriam Webster's Collegiate Dictionary Tenth Edition* (Springfield, MA: Merriam-Webster, Inc., 1996), p. 183.
2. MADD, "A Summary of Alcohol-Related Traffic Fatalities During the Holidays in 2001" [on-line], November 18, 2002. Available from: <http://www.madd.org/stats/0,1056,4906,00.html>.
3. Corrie ten Boom, various works [on-line], January 10, 2004, He First Loved Us. Available from: <http://www.hefirstlovedus.com/hefirstlovedus/Corrie_ten_Boom>.
4. Roy B. Zuch, *The Speaker's Quote Book* (Grand Rapids, MI: Kregel Publications, 1997), p. 386.
5. Ibid, p. 215.
6. Ibid, p. 216.
7. Ibid.

January

Hebrew: **Tebeth** (see Esther 2:16)

New Year's Day
January 1

Martin Luther King, Jr. Day
Third Monday in January

I will **celebrate** *before the* LORD.
(2 Samuel 6:21)

New Year's Day

Key Verse

Teach us to number our days aright,
that we may gain a heart of wisdom. (Psalm 90:12)

A Little History

Therefore, if anyone is in Christ, he is a new creation; the old has gone, the new has come!
(2 Corinthians 5:17)

In most of the world today, New Year's Day is celebrated on the first day of the first month of the year. One would think this would be the easiest of all holidays to remember, but through the ages, there has been much controversy about when the new year should actually begin.

In 46 BC, Roman emperor Julius Caesar proclaimed January 1 as New Year's Day. As the Roman Empire grew, its customs spread.[1] In fact, the month of January is named after the Roman god Janus, who is depicted with two faces, one looking back and the other looking forward.[2]

In an effort to shun the many pagan practices that had grown up around the celebration of the new year in January, church leaders in the Middle Ages changed the date. For many years, the first day of the year was considered to be March 25, which commemorates the day an angel announced to Mary that she would give birth to Jesus (see Luke 1:26-38). It wasn't until about 1600, when the revised Gregorian calendar gained widespread acceptance, that western nations once again began to celebrate the start of the new year on January 1.[3]

Today, most of the world, including the United States, celebrates New Year's Day on January 1. But there are some exceptions. The new year for Jewish people begins on Rosh Ha-Shanah, which is observed sometime in early fall (the actual day depends on the phases of the moon). Muslims use a calendar with 354 days (instead of 365), so the beginning of their new year fluctuates. For Hindus in India, the new year varies by region.[4]

The custom of making noise at the start of the new year was originally intended to drive away evil spirits. As Christianity spread, people instead would "make a joyful noise unto God" (Psalm 66:1, KJV) by cheering, banging pans, shooting muskets in the air and ringing church bells.[5] The custom of using the New Year's baby as a sign of fertility was also "reworked." Church leaders began to use the symbol of the baby to teach how we are "born again" through Jesus Christ.[6]

Making resolutions for the New Year is a popular tradition that is still practiced today. The custom dates back to the ancient Babylonians. Their most popular resolution was to return the farm implements they had borrowed from their neighbors.[7]

Many people, in the past and today, eat traditional foods as part of their New Year's celebrations. The French eat pancakes, the Swedes serve lutfisk in a cream sauce, the Dutch eat sauerkraut and southerners in the United States eat black-eyed peas.[8]

Another popular New Year's tradition is the singing of the Scottish melody "Auld Lang Syne" at the stroke of midnight. The song was first written down by Robert Burns in the 1700s. The song's title means "times gone by."[9]

While many people "ring in the New Year" with boisterous social events, some still carry on the tradition of a peaceful Watchnight Service. The custom was begun in the late eighteenth century by a Methodist congregation in Philadelphia. Members came together on New Year's Eve to praise God and pray for the coming year. At midnight, the church bells would ring and members would return home quietly.[10]

Many Christians still celebrate New Year's by attending a church service. Often, Holy Communion is served to emphasize that our past sins are forgiven. Through Jesus Christ we are given a brand new start for a brand new year!

A Closer Look

Therefore be careful how you walk, not as unwise men but as wise, making the most of your time. (Ephesians 5:15-16, NASB)

It's always interesting to see how crowded the health clubs and gyms are in January and then to watch how usage trickles back to normal by the end of the month. Although New Year's resolutions to either stop a bad habit or begin a good one are a popular tradition, most seem to be forgotten by February.

This year, instead of making New Year's resolutions, I have a challenge for you. Take the opportunity to look back, and ahead, to make sure you are using your time wisely. God calls us to "make the most of every opportunity" (Colossians 4:5), so it's clear that He cares about how we spend our time. We can show our love and devotion to Him by being good managers in this area.

Here's how to get started:

1. *Develop a mission statement.* Just as it is useless to run a race without knowing how to get to the finish line, it's foolish to aimlessly run through our lives. So, the first step in learning how to use our time wisely must be to prayerfully come before God to develop a mission statement.
2. *Set goals.* From your mission statement, develop a list of goals for the coming year. For example, you might want to gain more knowledge of the Bible, take better care of your health or reach out to the needy in the community. The key is to allow God to guide you in this process.

3. *Work out a game plan.* Now, from your goals, develop specific objectives. For example, to increase your knowledge of the Bible you might decide to read one chapter of the Bible a day, join a study group or memorize one verse a week. The key is to make your objectives specific, practical and measurable. In fact, I think it's best to make objectives for just one month at a time.
4. *Evaluate your schedule.* Use your goals and objectives to evaluate your schedule. What should you eliminate? Is there anything you need to add?
5. *Write it down.* Commit your plan to paper and put it in a prominent place (on the refrigerator, the bathroom mirror or the door to the garage—wherever you think you're most likely to see it). Every month or so, evaluate your plan.
6. *Pray and obey.* Just as you began the process prayerfully, conclude it the same way. Ask God to give you the wisdom, strength and determination to live a life worthy of the calling He has so graciously given you.

If their purpose or activity is of human origin, it will fail. (Acts 5:38)

Table Talk

- What are your favorite New Year's traditions or memories?
- Have you ever made any New Year's resolutions? Did you keep them?
- Do you have any resolutions for this year? What do you plan to do to keep them?
- How have you seen God at work in your life in the past year? What are some of the blessings you've received? How about lessons learned?
- How can you be a blessing to others in the coming year?

Celebrate!

Preschool and Above

- Tape several feet of "bubble wrap" to the floor or outside on the ground and allow children to jump on it. This is a fun yet safe alternative to fireworks.
- Use fabric paint to decorate a quilt square with a special memory from the previous year. Be sure to sign and date it. Quilt squares collected through the years could be sewn together to make a thoughtful gift when a child goes off to college or moves into a first home.
- Enjoy a cup of wassail (warm, spiced apple juice) and toast to each other's good health. (You can find the recipe for wassail on page 11.)
- Draw a picture with the four seasons. Then take it to a copy shop to be made into a calendar for the coming year. For a special touch add family birthdays and other special days to the calendar.

Elementary Age and Above

- Assemble a time capsule to be opened up in the future. Fill a strong, airtight container (e.g., coffee can, plastic tub or five-gallon bucket with a lid) with a variety of articles. You could include magazines, newspapers, playbills or ticket stubs, articles of trendy clothing, audio or videotapes of your family, photos, stamps, letters, postcards, etc. Place the items in zippered plastic bags, pack your container and then bury it or hide it away. Remember to include the date and names of those who put together the time capsule.
- Learn to say "Happy New Year!" in another language:
    Chinese: "Chu Shen Tan"
    French: "Bonne Annee"
    German: "Prosit Neujahr"
    Italian: "Felice Anno Nuovo"
    Spanish: "Feliz Año Nuevo"
    Sudanese: "Warsa Enggal"[11]
- Observe the Belgian tradition where children write and decorate notes to their parents and then read them out loud on New Year's Day. (Add a favorite Bible verse and/or blessing to make it even more special.)

Teens and Above

- Continue the New Year's tradition of Mother Lavender, a former slave who prepared dinners for the needy each New Year's Day to spread the love of Christ.[12] Continue her good works by serving dinner at a local homeless shelter or by collecting non-perishable items to stock your community food pantry. You could even enlist the help of a Sunday school or youth group.
- Prepare a dinner with a favorite family recipe as well as one you've never tried.
- Plan a "Watchnight Party." Share snacks and memories with family and friends as you wait for the new year to arrive. At midnight, spend some time praising God and asking for His guidance in the coming year.

Recipes to Enjoy

Wassail

Enjoy a cup of this spiced cider and toast to each other's good health!

2 quarts apple juice or cider
1 quart cranberry juice
1 t. whole spices (cloves, allspice)
2 cinnamon sticks

Tie the spices in a cheese cloth or put into a large tea ball. Add all ingredients to a large pot. Heat to boiling. Turn down heat and allow to steep on low for 30 minutes. Remove spices. Serve warm.

Hoppin' John

The first time my friend Linda presented me with a bag of black-eyed peas at our holiday party, I wasn't sure how to respond. Noticing the puzzled look on my face, she explained to this clueless northerner that Hoppin' John is a traditional New Year's food in the South.

1 cup uncooked rice
1/2 pound pork sausage
1/2 cup chopped onion
2 16-ounce cans black-eyed peas, drained
1 cup water
Salt and pepper to taste

Cook rice according to package directions. Brown sausage and onion. Drain fat. Add peas, water and seasoning. Simmer ten minutes, adding more water if needed.

Fondue Magic

Gathering around the fondue pot is a fantastic way to encourage conversation. It's also a simple way to entertain. Groovy, man!

Assorted vegetables cut into bite-sized pieces (baby carrots, zucchini, mushrooms, red onion, red, green or yellow peppers, peapods, etc.)
Assorted meat, chicken and/or fish cut into bite-sized pieces
Assorted bottled sauces (mustards, cocktail sauce, steak sauce, sweet and sour sauce, etc.)
Vegetable oil or vegetable broth
Electric fondue pot and forks

Assemble the vegetables and meat on separate platters. Put out small dishes of sauces. Heat the oil or broth in fondue pot. Put fondue pot in the middle of the table and instruct guests to use their fondue forks to spear and cook meat and vegetables. Dip in sauce before eating.

Martin Luther King, Jr. Day
Third Monday in January

Key Verse

There is neither Jew nor Greek, slave nor free, male nor female, for you are all one in Christ Jesus. (Galatians 3:28)

A Little History

Free at last, free at last!
Thank God Almighty, we are free at last![13]

Martin Luther King, Jr. Day honors a man who dedicated his life to seeing that all people, regardless of race, are treated equally under the law. A bill making the third Monday in January a federal holiday was signed by President Ronald Reagan on November 3, 1983. Dr. King, who is considered the undisputed leader of the civil rights movement, is one of the few social leaders in the world to be honored with a holiday.

Martin Luther King, Jr. was born in Atlanta, Georgia, in 1929. As a young African American growing up in the South, Martin (or M.L., as he was nicknamed) noticed that "black" people were treated differently than "white" people. As an African American, he could not use the same drinking fountains or restrooms as his white friends. And even though they lived in the same neighborhood, white kids went to a different school. Black people who rode buses were also expected to sit in the back of the bus and give up their seats to white people.[14]

After Martin finished his studies at Morehead University, he decided to attend Crozer Theological Seminary to become a Baptist minister like his father and grandfather. While in seminary, he met the woman who was to become his wife, Coretta Scott. After college, the young couple moved to Montgomery, Alabama, where Martin (now referred to as Dr. King) became the pastor of the Dexter Avenue Baptist Church.[15]

Shortly after accepting his new position, Dr. King was deeply troubled by the treatment of Rosa Parks, an African-American woman who was arrested for refusing to give her seat on the bus to a white man. Dr. King knew that Mrs. Parks was only one of many African-American men, women and children who faced injustice because of their skin color each day, and he wanted to do something to change it.[16]

While in seminary, Dr. King studied the concept of peaceful civil disobedience. He felt that if people would stand together and refuse to obey laws that were unjust, they could bring about change in a peaceful way. In response to the treatment of Mrs. Parks and other people, Dr. King convinced the African-American community to boycott the city bus system. As a result, the United States Supreme Court struck down Alabama's laws regarding bus segregation.[17]

Following this successful protest, Dr. King became known as a leader in the civil rights movement. In a typical year, he traveled 780,000 miles and made 208 speeches. His best known speech, "I Have a Dream," was given at a rally in Washington, DC, in 1963 to celebrate the 100th anniversary of the Emancipation Proclamation.[18]

In 1964, Dr. King was awarded the Nobel Peace Prize for his work.[19] And in 1965, President Lyndon Johnson signed a bill that Dr. King had fought very hard for: the Civil Rights Act. This law states that "no person in the United States shall, on the grounds of race, color, or national origin, be excluded from participation in, be denied the benefits of, or be subjected to discrimination."[20]

Dr. King continued in his fight against injustice, addressing groups across the nation. In April of 1968, he traveled to Memphis, Tennessee, to help with a strike by sanitation workers. It was there that he gave his last speech, declaring:

> Like anybody, I would like to live a long life. Longevity has its place. But I'm not concerned about that now. I just want to do God's will. And He's allowed me to go up to the mountain and see the Promised Land. And I'm not fearing any man. Mine eyes have seen the glory of the coming of the Lord![21]

The next day, as he was leaving his motel room, Dr. King was shot and killed by James Earl Ray.[22]

> *Those who hate me without reason*
> *outnumber the hairs of my head. (Psalm 69:4)*

A Closer Look

> *Have we not all one Father? Did not one God create us? Why do we profane the covenant of our fathers by breaking faith with one another? (Malachi 2:10)*

Martin Luther King, Jr. dedicated his life to bringing down the wall of racism that divided our nation. His dream was the same as that of our founding fathers, who wrote in the Declaration of Independence: "We hold these truths to be self-evident, that all men are created equal."[23]

Even as we celebrate the life of Dr. King, it's important to understand where his ideas were forged. It's not surprising that, as a Baptist minister, he drew many of his ideas directly from the Word of God. Consequently, this holiday provides a wonderful opportunity to learn what the Bible says about racism.

1. All men are created in the image of God.
   God created man in his own image. (Genesis 1:27)

2. We are all descendants of the first man and woman.

   From one man he made every nation of men. (Acts 17:26)

   Adam named his wife Eve, because she would become the mother of all the living. (Genesis 3:20)

3. All believers are brothers and sisters in Christ, regardless of race.

   There is neither Jew nor Greek, slave nor free, male nor female, for you are all one in Christ Jesus. (Galatians 3:28)

   You will not take pride in one man over against another. For who makes you different from anyone else? What do you have that you did not receive? And if you did receive it, why do you boast as though you did not? (1 Corinthians 4:6-7)

   Then Peter began to speak: "I now realize how true it is that God does not show favoritism but accepts men from every nation who fear him and do what is right." (Acts 10:34-35)

4. We are to treat fellow believers, regardless of race, with utmost dignity and respect.

   My brothers, as believers in our glorious Lord Jesus Christ, don't show favoritism. Suppose a man comes into your meeting wearing a gold ring and fine clothes, and a poor man in shabby clothes also comes in. If you show special attention to the man wearing fine clothes and say, "Here's a good seat for you," but say to the poor man, "You stand there" or "Sit on the floor by my feet," have you not discriminated among yourselves and become judges with evil thoughts? (James 2:1-4)

   God has shown me that I should not call any man impure or unclean. (Acts 10:28)

5. We are to love fellow believers, regardless of race.

   Anyone who claims to be in the light but hates his brother is still in the darkness. Whoever loves his brother lives in the light, and there is nothing in him to make him stumble. But whoever hates his brother is in the darkness and walks around in the darkness; he does not know where he is going, because the darkness has blinded him. (1 John 2:9-11)

As we can see, God has much to say about how we are to view and treat each other, no matter what shade of skin we are born with. A fitting tribute to both Dr. King and to God is a renewed commitment to tear down the walls of racism and allow the light of Jesus Christ to shine.

   *A fool finds no pleasure in understanding
      but delights in airing his own opinions. (Proverbs 18:2)*

Table Talk

• One of Martin Luther King, Jr.'s most famous speeches is called "I Have a Dream." What was his dream? What are your dreams for our world? For each of your kids?

- What do you think the word *racism* means? Do you think racism exists in our world today? If so, give some examples.
- How do you think God feels about racism among His people?
- What can you do to combat racism in our society?

Celebrate!

Preschool and Above

- Make a batch of "unity cookies" (you can find the recipe on page 17) and talk about how God can bring together many different things and produce a fabulous result. The same is true with His people!
- Do you have any friends of another race? If so, why not invite them over to play?

Elementary Age and Above

- Read or listen to Dr. King's historic "I Have a Dream" speech. (You can find a recording at your public library or on the Internet.) Afterwards, ask family members to share their dreams for our world.

Teens and Above

- Attend a worship service at a church with a congregation made up largely of people of a race different from your own. After the service, have a family discussion about similarities and differences when compared to your home congregation.
- Make a commitment to do something this year to combat racism in your community.

Recipes to Enjoy

"Tearin' Down the Walls" Pile-ups

When I first saw this recipe, I thought, Putting all these ingredients together can't work! They need to be separate! *Was I wrong! As my ten-year-old says, "This rocks, Mom!"*

It's even more fun to enjoy it with a crowd. Make the chicken sauce and rice ahead of time and ask each of your guests to bring one of the remaining ingredients. Put the ingredients in the order given on a buffet and have everyone make their own pile-ups! Trust me, it's a wonderful dish! (Serves 8-10)

To make chicken sauce, heat together:
    6 chicken breasts, cooked and cubed
    4 cans cream of chicken soup
    2 cups milk
Instruct guests to make their "pile-ups" by piling on ingredients in the order given:
    Chow mein noodles (1 bag)

White rice (2 1/2 cups rice, cooked)
Chicken sauce (see recipe above)
Tomatoes (2 cups, chopped)
Green onions (2 bunches, chopped)
Celery (2 cups chopped)
Crushed pineapple (2 16-ounce cans, drained)
Cheddar cheese (1 lb., grated)
Almonds (1/2 cup sliced)
Coconut (1/2 16-ounce bag, shredded)

Unity Cookies

These cookies have lots of different ingredients, but when mixed together, the result is fabulous! The same is true with God's people of all races.

1 cup brown sugar
1 cup white sugar
1 1/2 cups peanut butter
1/2 cup butter
3 eggs
2 t. vanilla
2 t. baking soda
4 1/2 cups oatmeal
3/4 cup chocolate chips
1/2 cup M&Ms

Cream together sugars, peanut butter and butter. Add eggs, vanilla and baking soda. Stir in oatmeal, chocolate chips and M&Ms. Drop by heaping teaspoonsful on a baking sheet. Flatten slightly. Bake at 350°F for 12-15 minutes. Makes about 5 dozen big cookies.

Notes

1. Lucille Recht Penner, *Celebration: The Story of American Holidays* (New York: Macmillan Publishing Company, 1993), p. 53.
2. Elizabeth Berg, *Family Traditions* (Pleasantville, NY: The Reader's Digest Association, 1992), p. 224.
3. Jerry Wilson, "It's Another New Year" [on-line], January 16, 2004. Available from: <http://wilstar.com/holidays/new-year.htm>.
4. Andrea Perry, "New Year's Celebrated Differently Around the World" [on-line], January 2, 2001. Available from: <http://www.ardmoreite.com/stories/010201/new_new_years.shtml>.
5. Penner, p. 55.
6. Wilson, "It's Another New Year."
7. Ibid.
8. Ibid.
9. Ibid.
10. Mamie R. Krythe, *All About American Holidays* (New York: Harper and Brothers, 1962), p. 16.

11. "New Year Wish Around the World" [on-line], November 23, 2002. Available from: <http://www.theholidayspot.com/newyear/wishes.htm>.

12. Malio Cardarelli, "Utica's Mother Lavender: I'll See You in Heaven" [on-line], January 16, 2004. Available from: <http://maliocard.tripod.com/book1.html>.

13. "The Holiday" [on-line], November 26, 2002. Available from: <http://www.holidays.net/mlk/holiday.htm>.

14. "The Rev. Dr. Martin Luther King, Jr." [on-line], November 26, 2002. Available from: <http://www.holidays.net/mlk/story.htm>.

15. Ibid.

16. Ibid.

17. Ibid.

18. Ibid.

19. Ibid., "The Holiday."

20. Ibid., "The Reverend Martin Luther King, Jr."

21. Ibid.

22. Ibid.

23. "The Declaration of Independence: A Transcription" [on-line], January 16, 2004. Available from: <http://www.archives.gov/national_archives_experience/declaration_transcript.html>.

February

Hebrew: **Shebat** (see Zechariah 1:7)

Groundhog Day
February 2

St. Valentine's Day
February 14

President's Day
Third Monday in February

Ash Wednesday and Lent
(see April holidays)

The whole assembly then agreed
to **celebrate** *. . . seven more days.*
(2 Chronicles 30:23)

Groundhog Day
February 2

Key Verse

Do any of the worthless idols of the nations bring rain?
Do the skies themselves send down showers?
No, it is you, O LORD our God.
Therefore our hope is in you,
for you are the one who does all this. (Jeremiah 14:22)

A Little History

If the sun shines on Groundhog Day;
Half the fuel and half the hay.[1]

When German settlers arrived in America during the 1700s, they brought with them a tradition known as Candlemas Day. Candlemas has its roots in a pagan celebration practiced in parts of Europe. Superstition held that if the weather was fair on February 2, which is halfway between winter and spring, the second half of winter would be stormy and cold.[2]

In the early Church, missionaries used many of the cultural practices of the people as a way to teach new Christians important truths about God (see 1 Corinthians 9:19-23). To teach the people that God controls the weather, the clergy began to bless candles and distribute them in the dark of winter. The lighted candles were placed in each window of a home on February 2 to signify that the occupants trusted God.[3] Unfortunately, the significance of Candlemas became muddled through the years. If the sun came out on February 2, the people took it as a sign from God that they could expect six more weeks of winter. If it was cloudy, they believed it was a sign that spring was just around the corner.[4]

When the Germans settled in Pennsylvania, they brought the celebration of Candlemas with them. To confirm that the day was sunny, people would look to see if an animal cast a shadow. The groundhog (also known as a woodchuck), waking from midwinter hibernation, was selected as the "official" shadow caster, and thus the name "Groundhog Day" came about.[5]

The earliest American reference to Groundhog Day can be found at the Pennsylvania Dutch Folklore Center at Franklin and Marshall College in a February 4, 1841, entry in Morgantown, Berks County (Pennsylvania), storekeeper James Morris' diary:

Last Tuesday, the 2nd, was Candlemas day, the day on which, according to the Germans, the Groundhog peeps out of his winter quarters and if he sees his shadow he pops back for another six weeks nap, but if the day be cloudy he remains out, as the weather is to be moderate.[6]

Pennsylvania's official celebration of Groundhog Day began on February 2, 1886, with a proclamation in *The Punxsutawney Spirit* by the newspaper's editor, Clymer Freas: "Today is Groundhog Day and up to the time of going to press the beast has not seen its shadow."[7] The groundhog was given the name "Punxsutawney Phil, Seer of Seers, Sage of Sages, Prognosticator of Prognosticators and Weather Prophet Extraordinary," and his hometown was thus called the "Weather Capital of the World."[8]

Today, Phil weighs fifteen pounds and thrives on dog food and ice cream in his climate-controlled home at the Punxsutawney Library. Each February 2, he is placed in a heated burrow underneath a simulated tree stump on a stage before being pulled out at 7:25 a.m. to make his prediction.[9] Since the 1993 release of the film *Groundhog Day*, attendance at the event has expanded. In 1997, there were 35,000 visitors in Punxsutawney, which is about five times the town's population.[10]

A Closer Look

Groundhog Day provides an excellent opportunity to share God's truth about such practices as divination, fortune-telling, sorcery and false prophets in a way that is not frightening to children. It's also a powerful reminder that, as Christians, we can trust God for our future.

The following Scripture verses may be helpful when talking about Groundhog Day:

Divination, Fortune-Telling

- Deuteronomy 18:14
- Jeremiah 23:33-40
- Jeremiah 27:9
- Ezekiel 13:22-23
- Zechariah 10:2
- Matthew 16:1-4
- Acts 16:16-18

Weather

- Psalm 135:6-7
- Jeremiah 51:15-16
- Mark 4:35-41

Future

- Jeremiah 29:11-13

Table Talk

- Why do you think people are so interested in knowing what's going to happen in the future?
- Do you think God wants us to worry about the future? Why or why not?
- Do you know anyone who has contacted a "psychic hot line" or who uses astrology or tarot cards? Do you think this is dangerous or just harmless fun? Why?
- (For parents) As a child, were you ever tempted by or did you know anyone who was involved in astrology or fortune-telling? What did you do?
- What should we, as Christians, do to help people we know who are involved in these practices?

Celebrate!

Preschool and Above

- Celebrate creation! Take a walk in your neighborhood once a week for the next six weeks. As you walk, look for signs of spring. Notice how God perfectly orchestrates the changing of the seasons. This is also a great time to praise God for His creation with singing. (Hymns and choruses like "Fairest Lord Jesus" and "Shout to the Lord" are great choices!)

Elementary and Above

Make a Cloud!
Stuff you'll need:
- warm water
- clear jar
- ice
- metal dish large enough to fit over opening of jar

Instructions: Place the ice in the metal dish. Let it stand until the dish gets very cold and then remove the ice. Then place one inch of very warm water in the jar. Place the metal dish over the top of the jar. As the warm water evaporates, it meets the cold dish. The moisture will condense and form a cloud.

Catch a Snowflake!
Stuff you'll need:
- black velvet or black construction paper
- magnifying glass
- snow

Instructions: Freeze your cloth or paper. Have the cloth or paper frozen and ready to go for the next snowfall. Place the cloth or paper outside and let some snowflakes land on the dark surface. Quickly, before they melt, examine the snowflakes with a magnifying glass. Many snowflakes are "broken" and so you don't see the whole six-sided crystal, but with persistence you'll see some beautiful examples.

Teenagers and Above

• Be a super sleuth! Use the Internet to check the weather log in your area and/or other areas for the last decade. Chart conditions and temperatures for the six weeks following February 2. Do the superstitions surrounding Groundhog Day hold up scientifically?

Recipes to Enjoy

Groundhog Stew

1 lb. lean hamburger
1/2 cup chopped onions
2 t. chopped garlic
1 16-ounce bag frozen mixed vegetables
1 16-ounce can chopped tomatoes, undrained
1 16-ounce can kidney beans, drained
1 cup vegetable juice (V-8, etc.)
1 t. oregano
1 t. marjoram
1 t. thyme
1 t. sugar

Brown hamburger with garlic and onions until fully cooked. Drain any accumulated grease. Add remaining ingredients and simmer 30-45 minutes. Add salt and pepper to taste. Serve with crusty bread and a salad. (Note: Be sure to keep proof that the meat in the stew is not truly "groundhog" or your family may boycott dinner.)

Weatherman's Favorite Cupcakes

1 dozen unfrosted cupcakes baked in paper liners
1 can prepared frosting, white
Yellow food coloring
2 cups shredded coconut
A variety of decorating items (such as raisins, fruit roll-ups or snacks, licorice, trail mix, sprinkles, decorating frosting, etc.)

Tint half the frosting and half the shredded coconut with yellow food coloring. Frost six cupcakes with tinted frosting and sprinkle with tinted coconut. Do the same with the other six cupcakes using white frosting and untinted coconut. Decorate the cupcakes as snowmen or sunbursts. These treats will put a smile on your face regardless of the weather!

St. Valentine's Day

Key Verse

Dear children, let us not love with words or tongue but with actions and in truth. (1 John 3:18)

A Little History

There are several accounts about who was the true inspiration for St. Valentine's Day. My favorite is about a Christian in the early Church named Valentine, who was arrested because he refused to pray to the Roman gods. While in prison, he formed a close friendship with a prison guard and his blind daughter.

After many years, Valentine was called before the Roman emperor Claudius II, also known as Claudius the Cruel. Claudius offered Valentine freedom if he would renounce his faith. Valentine refused, even going so far as to share the good news of the gospel with the emperor in an effort to convert him to Christianity.

Claudius the Cruel flew into a rage and ordered Valentine beheaded. Legend has it that before he was taken to the guillotine, Valentine asked his friend, the prison guard, to give a note to his daughter. As the girl opened the letter, her sight was miraculously restored and she was able to read the note which was signed, "From your Valentine."[11]

A Closer Look

Jesus replied: "'Love the Lord your God with all your heart and with all your soul and with all your mind.' This is the first and greatest commandment. And the second is like it: 'Love your neighbor as yourself.' All the Law and the Prophets hang on these two commandments." (Matthew 22:37-40)

The story of strong faith and friendship that is the inspiration for Valentine's Day brings new meaning to a holiday which often isolates those who may not be involved in a romantic relationship. This holiday is a celebration of the love of a man willing to give up his very life rather than betray God. His story also brings to mind the great love Jesus demonstrated for us by giving up His life so that we may have access to eternal life (see John 3:16).

Valentine's Day also gives us an opportunity to reach out to those around us with the love of Christ. Who in your circle of influence could use a word or touch to show that he is loved? Perhaps it's a widow in your neighborhood or a single mother who is struggling to care for her children. Maybe it's a coworker or a veteran living in a nursing home. Who can you encourage this Valentine's Day?

The Bible uses the words *love*, *loves* or *loved* 721 times. Do you think God might be trying to tell us something? The following are just a few verses about love that will encourage and inspire you:

- Psalm 116:1
- Psalm 136:1
- Proverbs 3:3
- Hosea 6:4
- Matthew 3:17
- Mark 12:30-31
- John 3:16
- John 14:15
- Romans 12:10
- 1 Corinthians 13
- Galatians 5:22
- Philemon 7

Table Talk

- What do you think it means, in practical terms, to love God with all our hearts, with all our souls and with all our minds? Give some specific examples.
- What do you think it means to love another person as yourself? Give specific examples.
- Who in your life do you need to reach out to in brotherly love? How will you do it?

Celebrate!

Preschool and Above

- Use soap to draw a special message to your loved one(s) on the bathroom mirror. Craft stores even have special soap "crayons" that would be perfect for this.

Elementary and Above

- Write a special Bible verse about God's love for us on red hearts with gold ink and set one on each family member's dinner plate or tuck it into their lunch boxes.

A Transparent Heart

Often when we allow others to see inside our hearts, they in turn begin to open up. This fun craft can serve as a beautiful reminder to have a transparent heart.

Stuff you'll need:
- waxed paper
- several crayons
- small hand-held pencil sharpener
- iron
- craft paper (or any kind of plain paper)
- hole punch
- thin ribbon
- scissors

Instructions: Pull off a sheet of waxed paper and fold it in half. On one half of the paper, evenly sprinkle crayon shavings. (You can make the shavings by using a small hand-held pencil sharpener.) Then carefully fold the other half in place and place a sheet of craft paper under and on top of it. Press with a warm iron to melt the crayon shavings and fuse the waxed paper together. You can now cut the paper into heart shapes. Use the hole punch to make a hole at the top center and tie with a thin satin ribbon for hanging. These translucent hearts look especially pretty in front of a window.

Teenager and Above

- Practice a "random act of kindness" by giving someone your place in line or by paying for the lunch of the person behind you in the drive-thru.

Recipes to Enjoy

- Shape your favorite Rice Krispie treat recipe to look like a big Hershey's kiss by using a funnel as a mold. You can use Cocoa Krispies for a chocolate kiss. Package by twisting foil around the kiss. The "tag" can be a Bible verse about love (Jeremiah 31:3 is a great choice).
- Make heart-shaped pancakes or waffles for breakfast. You can use a pancake mold or you can try this method: Put pancake batter in a plastic bag, snip off the corner, pipe the batter in the outline of a heart on a hot griddle and then fill in the middle. You can serve strawberries on the side. When sliced, strawberries look like little hearts!
- My friend Kim likes to serve a completely red meal on Valentine's Day: spaghetti with heart-shaped meatballs, strawberries, red milk and red velvet cake. I think she even tints her garlic bread red!
- Use a cookie cutter to cut heart shapes from a pan of brownies. Frost with pink frosting and decorate with candy hearts or sprinkles. (Many Christian bookstores now carry candy hearts with Christian messages around Valentine's Day. How fun!)

President's Day

3rd Monday in February

Key Verse

For lack of guidance a nation falls. (Proverbs 11:14)

A Little History

President's Day honors two of America's most famous presidents: George Washington and Abraham Lincoln. They were both born in February: Washington was born on February 22, 1732, and Lincoln on February 12, 1809. In 1971, Congress declared a federal holiday to honor both men.[12]

Washington and Lincoln may not have shared a birthday, but they did have much in common. Both men led the United States through two of the most difficult times in our history: the Revolutionary War and the Civil War. Both men also came from humble beginnings and did not seek their positions, but accepted them due to a sense of duty to their country. Most important, both George Washington and Abraham Lincoln were known as men of extremely high integrity that was born from an unwavering faith in God.

One of the most famous stories about George Washington is one that some historians say may not be true. It tells of young George cutting down a cherry tree and, when asked by his father if he had done it, replying, "I cannot tell a lie. I cut down the cherry tree." Although this story may not be true, it emphasizes the importance our first President placed on telling the truth.[13]

A story that is not as well-known, but which is documented to be true, concerns Washington's early military service in the French and Indian War when America was still a British colony. After a battle in which 714 American and British soldiers were shot down, Washington wrote in a letter to his brother, "Dear Jack, I am writing to assure you that I am still alive by the miraculous care of Providence that protected me beyond all human expectation. I found four bullet holes in my coat and two horses were shot from under me. Yet I escaped unhurt."[14] Until the 1960s, this story was found in the majority of public school textbooks.[15]

When Colonel George Washington was selected to take command of the Continental Army in the Revolutionary War, he said with tears in his eyes, "I do not have the training for such an important command." After the United States won freedom from England, Washington refused to take credit for the victory. "The hand of Providence has been so clear in the course of this war," he wrote in a letter to another general. "A man would have to be worse than an atheist not to gratefully admit God's help."[16]

When Washington was sworn in as the first President of the United States, he added four of his own words to the end of the oath: "So help me, God."[17]

Abraham Lincoln, a man who grew up in a log "lean-to" in the woods of Kentucky and spent just one year in school, was inaugurated as our sixteenth president during one of the most tumultuous times in our nation's history.[18] It was not a position Lincoln sought lightly, as evidenced in his comments upon leaving Illinois for Washington, DC.

> I now leave, not knowing when or if I will return. The task before me is greater than that which rested upon Washington. Without the help of that Divine Being who always helped him, I cannot succeed. With God's help, I cannot fail. Trusting in Him who can go with me, and remain with you, and be everywhere for good, let us confidently hope that all will yet be well.[19]

Shortly after Lincoln took office, the Confederate Army fired on Fort Sumter and the Civil War officially began. Although Lincoln had hoped for a speedy victory, the war dragged on. He wrote one day, "I am almost ready to say that this war is God's will and that He's not ready for it to end yet. It is quite possible that God's purpose is something different from the purpose of either side in this battle."[20]

As Lincoln continued to read his Bible and pray, he felt more and more that God's purpose for the war was to end the practice of slavery. Lincoln asked all Americans to spend a day in prayer and fasting. "Since we know that nations are subject to God's correction, we must consider that this awful civil war may be punishment for our sins." On September 22, 1862, Lincoln issued a proclamation freeing the slaves.[21]

As the Union army marched into Pennsylvania for the battle of Gettysburg, Lincoln knelt to pray for God's protection from another horrible defeat. Lincoln told a friend that a feeling of comfort came over him. "It was as if God Almighty had taken the whole business into His own hands and that things would go all right at Gettysburg."

After the North's victory at Gettysburg, the Confederate Army never regained its strength. In Lincoln's famous Gettysburg Address, he said:

> It is for us, the living, to dedicate ourselves to the unfinished work which they who fought here have so bravely advanced. . . . Let us make sure that these dead shall not have died in vain—that this nation, under God, shall have a new birth of freedom—and that government of the people, by the people, for the people, shall not perish from the earth.[22]

There are two memorials in Washington, DC, which honor these great leaders. The Washington Monument rises 555 feet tall and is reflected in the Potomac River. At the top is inscribed "Praise be to God," which seems to sum up the attitude of this great man who trusted God in all he did.[23]

Inscribed on the wall of the Lincoln Memorial are the powerful words from Abraham Lincoln's second Inaugural address, spoken just weeks before he was assassinated.

> With malice toward none; with charity for all; with firmness in the right, as God gives us to see the right, let us strive on to finish the work we are in; to bind up the nation's

wounds; to care for his widow and his orphan—to do all which may achieve and cherish a just and lasting peace among ourselves and with all nations.[24]

A Closer Look

If you do not stand firm in your faith,
you will not stand at all. (Isaiah 7:9)

Among the things that made Lincoln and Washington great leaders are not only the challenges they faced, but their strong moral characters born from steadfast faith in God. Both men possessed and demonstrated a clear sense of right and wrong and a commitment to follow the right path.

In George Washington's farewell address in 1796, our first President proclaimed,

> Reason and experience both forbid us to expect that national morality can prevail in exclusion of religious principle. Morality is a necessary spring of popular government. Of all the dispositions and habits which lead to political prosperity, religion and morality are indispensable supports. In vain would that man claim the tribute of patriotism who should labor to subvert these great pillars of human happiness, these firmest props of the duties of men and citizens.[25]

Washington felt this message was so important to Americans that he took the unprecedented step of having the entire text of his address published in newspapers throughout the nation to make sure all citizens had a chance to read it.[26]

Today, although we still celebrate President's Day, indications are that Americans are no longer heeding Washington's words. During the impeachment trial of our forty-second President, William Jefferson Clinton, Americans were asked if they felt character was crucial to sound leadership. An alarming majority of Americans, buoyed by a strong economy, responded that they did not feel that good character was necessary for the President to do a good job. It's interesting to note that lack of "morality" and "character" by leaders in the corporate world (as evidenced by the Enron and WorldCom scandals) sent Wall Street into chaos and led to the loss of savings built up by the "strong" economy. I wonder how many Americans feel that the character of our leaders is irrelevant today.

As Abraham Lincoln said, "You cannot have the right to do what is wrong."[27]

Table Talk

- What character traits do you think are important for the leaders of our country to have? Why?
- What character traits, from what you now know about George Washington and Abraham Lincoln, impress you most? Why? Which of these traits would you like to cultivate in your own life? How will you do this?

- Do you think strong faith in God is an important prerequisite for our government leaders? Why or why not?
- What can we, as citizens, do to choose good leaders?

Celebrate!

Preschool and Above

- Build a log cabin from pretzel rods. Use peanut butter as "mortar" and snack crackers to shingle the roof. This works best if you build your cabin around a half-pint milk carton to support the structure.

Elementary and Above

- Visit a memorial to a leader in your community. Why was the memorial constructed? What made this person great?

Teenagers and Above

- Commit to praying for our government leaders on a regular basis. You can receive specific prayer requests from the President and his staff by joining the Presidential Prayer Team at www.presidentialprayerteam.org or by contacting: The Presidential Prayer Team, PO Box 2300, Orange, CA 92859, 520.797.7173. There is no cost to join, other than a commitment to pray.

Recipes to Enjoy

Bake cherry muffins or a cherry dessert in honor of our first President's honesty. Even though there's no proof that the cherry tree story really happened, it's a good reminder of the importance God places on honesty (see Exodus 20:16).

Deb's Cherry Coffee Cake Bars

1 cup butter or margarine, softened
1 1/2 cups sugar
4 eggs
1 t. vanilla
3 cups flour
2 1/2 t. baking powder
1/2 t. salt
1 can cherry pie filling
Icing (see recipe below)

Preheat oven to 300°F. Cream softened butter and sugar. Add eggs one at a time, mixing after each addition. Add vanilla. Mix dry ingredients in a separate bowl and then add gradually to butter and sugar mixture. Spread 2/3 of this mixture on a 10 x 13-inch cookie sheet. Drop pie filling, then remaining batter on mixture. Bake 30-45 minutes until slightly golden. While warm, drizzle icing over it.

For icing, mix together until smooth: 1 cup powdered sugar, 1 t. vanilla, 1 T. water

Cyndy's Cherry Pie

1 deep-dish pie shell, unbaked
1 large can cherry pie filling
1/2 cup brown sugar
1/2 cup flour
1/2 cup chopped pecans
3 T. butter or margarine, melted

Dump the pie filling into the shell. Mix together the brown sugar, flour, butter and pecans with a pastry cutter or food processor. Sprinkle over the top of the pie. Bake at 350°F for 30 minutes.

Notes

1. "Stormfax Weather Almanac" [on-line], January 20, 2004. Available from: <http://www.stormfax.com/ghogday. htm>.
2. Ibid.
3. Bill Anderson, "Groundhog Day: 1886-1992" [on-line], January 16, 2004. Available from: <http://www.groundhog. org/>.
4. Ibid.
5. Ibid.
6. "Stormfax Weather Almanac."
7. Anderson.
8. "Stormfax Weather Almanac."
9. Ibid.
10. Ibid.
11. "Saint Valentine" [on-line], August 18, 2002. January 26, 2000. Available from: <http://www.maxpages.com/stvalentine/Saint_Valentine>.
12. "President's Day History" [on-line], January 20, 2004. Available from: <http://holidays.huddlenet.com/president/history.shtml>.
13. "Learning About George Washington" [on-line], January 20, 2004. Available from: <http://gwpapers.virginia.edu/lesson/k5/k5slide5.html>.
14. Timothy Crater and Ranelda Hunsicker, *In God We Trust: Stories of Faith in American History* (Colorado Springs, CO: Cook Communications, 1997), p. 96.
15. David Barton, *America's Godly Heritage* (Aledo, TX: Wallbuilders Press, 1993), p. 3.
16. Crater and Hunsicker.
17. Ibid.
18. "Lawyer's Hall of Fame: Abraham Lincoln" [on-line], January 21, 2004. Available from: <http://www.fansoffieger.com/lincoln.htm>.
19. Crater and Hunsicker, p. 172.
20. Ibid, p. 173.
21. Ibid.
22. Os Guiness, *Character Counts* (Grand Rapids, MI: Baker Book House, 1999), p.130.
23. Ibid, p. 175.
24. Carol Barkin and Elizabeth James, *The Holiday Handbook* (New York: Clarion Books, 1994), p. 97.

25. George Washington's Farewell Address, as compiled by James D. Richardson, *Messages and Papers of the Presidents, 1789-1897* (Bureau of National Literature 1913, 1897), 1:205-216.
26. Ibid.
27. Gene Griessman, *The Words Lincoln Lived By: 52 Timeless Principles To Light Your Path* (New York: Fireside/ Simon & Schuster, 2000), p. 113.

March

Hebrew: **Adar** (see Esther 3:7)

St. Patrick's Day
March 17

Holy Week and Easter
(see April holidays)

So they began to **celebrate***. (Luke 15:24)*

St. Patrick's Day
March 17

Key Verse

Therefore go and make disciples of all nations, baptizing them in the name of the Father and of the Son and of the Holy Spirit, and teaching them to obey everything I have commanded you. (Matthew 28:19-20)

A Little History

Many stories, from driving away snakes to raising people from the dead, have grown up around the life of the man honored on St. Patrick's Day. But the true story of Patrick, written in his own hand shortly before his death, gives us a glimpse into the heart of a simple man who loved God deeply and had a passion to share His love with others.[1]

Patrick, originally named Maewyn, was born in Wales around AD 385. He was the son of a deacon of the Christian Church and the grandson of an elder. Although born into a family that professed a strong faith, Patrick wrote that he had little use for God. At the age of sixteen, he was kidnapped and sold into slavery as a herdsman in Hibernia, which is now Ireland.[2] In his *Confession*, Patrick wrote that it was during his captivity that God began to work in his heart.

> And there the Lord opened my mind to an awareness of my unbelief, in order that, even so late, I might remember my transgressions and turn with all my heart to the Lord my God, who had regard for my insignificance and pitied my youth and ignorance. And he watched over me before I knew him, and before I learned sense or even distinguished between good and evil, and he protected me, and consoled me as a father would his son.[3]

Patrick spent his early years in Ireland tending sheep for his captors. He says during those years he came to truly know and love God.

> But after I reached Hibernia, I used to pasture the flock each day and I used to pray many times a day. More and more did the love of God, and my fear of him and faith increase, and my spirit was moved so that in a day [I said] from one up to a hundred prayers, and in the night a like number; besides I used to stay out in the forests and on the mountain and I would wake up before daylight to pray in the snow, in icy coldness, in rain, and I used to feel neither ill nor any slothfulness, because, as I now see, the Spirit was burning in me at that time.[4]

In his *Confession*, Patrick wrote that during the sixth year of his captivity he had a dream telling him that he should flee and directing him to a boat to ferry him back to Britain. Once safely home with his family, he had another dream directing him to return to Ireland, this time as a missionary to the people. At that point in history, Ireland was a pagan country steeped in Druidism, a religion that worshipped idols and conducted human sacrifices. Both family members and Patrick's church family tried to convince him not to return to Ireland. Seeing that he was not concerned for his safety, elders tried to convince him that he was not worthy of such a calling because of his past sins and lack of education. Patrick was not swayed.

> Thus I give untiring thanks to God who kept me faithful in the day of my temptation, so that today I may confidently offer my soul as a living sacrifice for Christ my Lord; who am I, Lord? or, rather, what is my calling? that you appeared to me in so great a divine quality, so that today among the barbarians I might constantly exalt and magnify your name in whatever place I should be, and not only in good fortune, but even in affliction? So that whatever befalls me, be it good or bad, I should accept it equally, and give thanks always to God who revealed to me that I might trust in him.[5]

Although he faced many trials and almost lost his life several times, Patrick worked diligently to spread the good news of Jesus Christ to the Irish people. In turn, he developed a strong love for those to whom he ministered and was able to witness the spread of faith and the establishment of Christian churches throughout the land. Patrick died on March 17, AD 465, but not without issuing a strong exhortation through his *Confession* to all who feel the calling to be missionaries in foreign and dangerous lands.

> One should, in fact, fish well and diligently, just as the Lord foretells and teaches, saying, "Follow me, and I will make you fishers of men" [Matthew 4:19, KJV], and again through the prophets: "Behold, I am sending forth many fishers and hunters, says the Lord [see Jeremiah 16:16, KJV]," et cetera. So it behooved us to spread our nets, that a vast multitude and throng might be caught for God, and so there might be clergy everywhere who baptized and exhorted a needy and desirous people.[6]

Patrick's beliefs, expressed in his *Confession,* follow right along with Scriptures such as Matthew 28:19, which says: "Therefore go and make disciples of all nations, baptizing them in the name of the Father and of the Son and of the Holy Spirit," and Mark 16:15, which says: "Go into all the world and preach the good news to all creation."

A Closer Look

After reading the passionate words of St. Patrick, whose heart was set on the single purpose of spreading the light of Jesus Christ in a dark world, I just wanted to weep. I weep with joy that God has raised up people like Patrick with such missionary zeal and that He continues to do so. But I also weep with sorrow to see what has become of the day set aside to honor the work of Patrick of Ireland. As Christians, we can take back this holiday by passing on the true story of St. Patrick to future generations.

It's said that Patrick, like the Apostle Paul, used elements from the culture of the people he was ministering to as a way of explaining important truths of God. Legend has it that he used the shamrock, native to Ireland, to help people understand the Trinity.[7] In families today, we have the opportunity to use the symbols associated with the celebration of St. Patrick's Day to impress upon our children the true passion of Patrick of Ireland. For example:

- It's said that Patrick drove the snakes from Ireland.[8] There are many instances in Scripture where Satan is depicted as a serpent (see Genesis 3; Revelation 12:9, 15; 20:2). As Patrick spread the gospel of Jesus Christ among the Druids, he was driving out the influence of Satan.
- The rainbow with a pot of gold is a common symbol used in conjunction with St. Patrick's Day. God set a rainbow in the sky as a reminder to His people of His promise never to destroy the earth with water. The throne of God in heaven is also described as being encircled by a rainbow (see Revelation 4:3). The pot of gold can be used to teach of the treasures God has promised His people (see Matthew 13:44; 19:21; Mark 10:21; Luke 12:33-34; 18:22 and many others).
- Leprechauns are mythical creatures charged with making the shoes of fairies. They were supposed to live alone and were greedy, cranky little men known for lying and cheating others. The legend is that if a leprechaun is caught, he will try to buy his freedom by leading his captor to his hidden pot of gold.[9] Leprechauns offer a treasure trove of conversation starters on the subjects of greed, lying and stealing.

Table Talk!

- How are people today sometimes like leprechauns?
- What is in your "pot o' gold"?
- Why do you think the true story of St. Patrick has been lost in today's culture?
- What symbols in today's culture could you use to share the good news of Jesus with those who don't know Him?

Celebrate!

Preschool and Above

- Sprinkle gold coins on a table (chocolate coins are both fun and delicious!) and talk about how we can store up treasure in heaven (see Matthew 6:19-20).

Elementary and Above

- Deliver a shamrock plant to a friend with a Bible verse and/or the true story of St. Patrick attached to it.

- Send a care package to encourage a missionary.

Teenagers and Above

- Prepare and serve a completely green meal (pea soup, green salad, green bread, green milk and, of course, pistachio ice cream for dessert!).

Recipes to Enjoy

Salzmanns' Favorite Corned Beef and Cabbage

2 cups baby carrots
3 lb. (approx.) corned beef brisket
2 onions, quartered
1 cup water
1 small head cabbage, cored and cut in wedges

Put the carrots in a slow cooker, then meat, then onions. Pour water on top and cook on low for 8-10 hours (or on high for 5-6 hours). During the last 2-3 hours (1 1/2 hours if cooking on high), add cabbage, pressing down into liquid. Serve with boiled new potatoes, if desired. Enjoy!

Blarney Stones

These treats are not only fun to make and taste good, they are great conversation starters! Explain how people from all over the world travel to a castle in Ireland to kiss a big, moss-covered rock for good luck. While you enjoy the treats, talk about how true "good luck" and protection comes from the One who created the rock: God Almighty (see Psalm 46:1-7).

Using your favorite Rice Krispie treat recipe, add green food coloring to the marshmallow mixture before stirring into the cereal. Instead of squares, mound the treats on waxed paper so they look like rocks. The treats will be ready to eat in 30 minutes (or less if you don't care about green, sticky hands!).

Notes

1. Ralph Wilson, "Christian Articles Archive: Patrick's Confession" [on-line], August 21, 2002. Available from: <http://www.joyfulheart.com>.
2. Ibid.
3. Ibid.
4. Ibid.
5. Ibid.
6. Ibid.
7. Jerry Wilson, "St. Patrick's Day: Customs and Traditions" [on-line], 1999, August 9, 2002. Available from: <http://www.wilstar.net/holidays/patrick.htm>.
8. Ibid.
9. "Irish Symbols: Leprechaun" [on-line], January 21, 2004. Available from: <http://www.occdsb.on.ca/~proj8169/irish-symbols-leprechaun.htm>.

April

Hebrew: **Abib** (see Exodus 13:4)

April Fool's Day
April 1

Easter Season
February-April

Lent	Begins forty-six days before Easter, ends the day before Easter
Ash Wednesday	First day of Lent, seven Wednesdays before Easter
Palm Sunday	Sunday immediately before Easter Sunday
Maundy Thursday	Thursday immediately before Easter Sunday
Good Friday	Friday immediately before Easter Sunday
Holy Saturday/Easter Vigil	Saturday immediately before Easter Sunday
Easter Sunday	Celebrated on the Sunday after the first full moon on or after the first day of spring; can occur between March 22 and April 25

Celebrate *and be glad. (Luke 15:32)*

April Fool's Day
April 1

Key Verse

A cheerful heart is good medicine. (Proverbs 17:22)

A Little History

Since April Fool's is a holiday with a lot of laughing, it's only fitting that its origin be a bit goofy. For centuries the people of France observed New Year's Day on April 1. The holiday was celebrated in much the same way as it is today, with late-night parties ringing in the New Year.[1]

In 1562, Pope Gregory decided to change the date of New Year's to January 1. (The reason for this is too complicated to talk about on such a silly holiday, but it has something to do with the lunar cycles, etc. You can find out more about this by researching the Gregorian calendar.) Anyway, many people in France hadn't heard about the change or chose not to believe that the Pope would actually change the date of New Year's. They decided to continue celebrating New Year's on April 1. These stubborn people became known as the first April fools.[2]

Since then, April 1 has become a day for playing tricks on friends or family members. In France, children would tape a paper fish on their schoolmates' backs. When the child would discover the fish, the trickster would yell, "Poisson d'Avvil!" or "April Fish!"[3] In the nineteenth century, American schoolteachers would try to trick their students by saying, "Look! A flock of geese!" When the children looked to the sky, the teacher would say, "April fool!"[4]

Today, the holiday is celebrated in much the same way, with tricks and practical jokes. There are probably few adults who haven't been fooled by the, "Look, your shoe's untied!" trick on April Fool's Day. Other common pranks include putting salt in the sugar bowl and setting clocks back in a home.

April Fool's Day is a favorite holiday for people who like to play practical jokes, including my normally placid husband. One year, John fooled the family by bringing home a dozen doughnuts filled with mustard instead of jelly. I have to admit, the look on our teenagers' faces as they dug into the doughnuts proves that laughter is, indeed, good medicine!

A Closer Look

The fool says in his heart,
  "There is no God." (Psalm 14:1)

April Fool's Day provides an excellent opportunity to have a little fun as well as a chance to talk about what it really means to be a "fool." The book of Proverbs alone has seventy-five references concerning fools and foolishness! Here are just a few:

- "A chattering fool comes to ruin." (10:10)
- "A fool finds pleasure in evil conduct." (10:23)
- "The fool will be servant to the wise." (11:29)
- "A fool shows his annoyance at once." (12:16)
- "A fool is hotheaded and reckless." (14:16)
- "A fool spurns his father's discipline." (15:5)
- "To have a fool for a son brings grief." (17:21)
- "A fool repeats his folly." (26:11)
- "He who trusts in himself is a fool." (28:26)
- "The fool rages and scoffs." (29:9)

April Fool's Day also offers an opportunity to talk about how God considers a fool the one who intentionally or unthinkingly hurts another person with his joke or prank.

> *May the words of my mouth and the meditation of my heart*
> *be pleasing in your sight,*
> *O Lord, my Rock and my Redeemer. (Psalm 19:14)*

Finally, it's important, especially when talking to children, to distinguish between foolishness and immaturity. The Bible calls those who are full of pride and spiritually blind "fools" (Matthew 23:17) as opposed to those who may have little knowledge of spiritual things but are seeking the way of the Lord.

> *Do not forsake wisdom, and she will protect you;*
> *love her, and she will watch over you. (Proverbs 4:6)*

Table Talk

- What makes you laugh?
- Has anyone ever played a practical joke on you? What was it? How did it make you feel?
- What are some of the characteristics of a "fool" in today's culture? What can we do to avoid becoming a "fool" or doing "foolish" things?

Celebrate!

All Ages

- Instead of making someone an "April fool," how about reaching out to someone who needs a little encouragement to make him an "April friend" instead? Bring dinner to a single mom. Lead a sing-along with your children at a retirement community. Drop off a bouquet of daffodils to a widow. Bake cookies or send a note of encouragement to your church staff. Look around; God will bring an "April friend" to a willing heart!

Elementary and Above

• Add a little laughter to your daily routine. You can receive a free and clean "laugh a day" by e-mail by contacting www.laugh-a-lot.com. The Christian Humor Hotline at www. angelfire.com/ca4/HumorHotline/ is also a great place to take a "smile break."

Recipes to Enjoy

Berry Fool

A "fool" is a simple English dessert made by mixing whipped cream or custard with sweetened crushed fruit. This version uses berries, but you can also use any kind of soft fruit—bananas, mango, passion fruit, kiwi, peaches, apricots, etc. Trust me; even a kitchen "fool" will be a hit with this easy dish!

> 2 cups heavy whipping cream
> 2 cups berries (strawberries, raspberries or blackberries)
> Sugar to taste (about 1/4 cup)

Sprinkle the sugar on the berries and crush the fruit with a fork or pastry blender. Beat the cream in a chilled bowl with whisk or electric mixer until it forms soft peaks. Gently stir in the fruit. It should look kind of "striped" by the crushed fruit, not completely mixed in. Chill until serving time. Enjoy!

Easter Season
February-April

Lent	Begins forty-six days before Easter, ends the day before Easter
Ash Wednesday	First day of Lent, seven Wednesdays before Easter
Palm Sunday	Sunday immediately before Easter Sunday
Maundy Thursday	Thursday immediately before Easter Sunday
Good Friday	Friday immediately before Easter Sunday
Holy Saturday/Easter Vigil	Saturday immediately before Easter Sunday
Easter Sunday	Celebrated on the Sunday after the first full moon on or after the first day of spring; can occur between March 22 and April 25

Key Verse

For God so loved the world that he gave his one and only Son, that whoever believes in him shall not perish but have eternal life. (John 3:16)

A Little History

The Easter season, which commemorates Jesus' death and resurrection, is the most important Christian festival of the entire year. Easter is the day when Christians gather to celebrate the resurrection of our Lord and Savior. For centuries, some have attempted to dilute the true significance of this important season by tying it to pagan practices. We'll first take a look at the intended meaning and historical significance of the Easter holidays and then at some ways to keep the focus on Jesus.

The Easter holidays consist of a season of preparation (Ash Wednesday, Lent), commemoration of the events of the week before Jesus' resurrection (Palm Sunday, Maundy Thursday, Good Friday and Easter Vigil) and, of course, a joyous celebration of Jesus rising from the dead (Easter Sunday). All of the parts of the Easter holiday have had special meaning to Christians throughout history.

Lent

Repent and believe the good news! (Mark 1:15)

Lent is the symbolic remembrance of the forty days Jesus spent in the wilderness to prepare for His ministry. Lent actually begins forty-six days (not forty days) before Easter. Sundays, which are feast days, are not considered to be part of Lent.[5]

During this time, Christians are encouraged to examine their lives and repent of sin. Some denominations practice forms of self-denial during Lent, such as giving up certain foods or activities. For example, many of my Roman Catholic friends give up meat on Fridays. Most churches also hold special midweek services during Lent.

Ash Wednesday

For dust you are
and to dust you will return. (Genesis 3:19)

The Lenten season begins on Ash Wednesday, forty-six days before Easter Sunday.[6] Although the practice of placing ashes on one's head or face during Lent was practiced in the early Church, Ash Wednesday wasn't declared an "official" holiday until the Synod of Benevento in AD 1091.[7]

Throughout the Bible, ashes are used as a symbol of repentance and purification (see Numbers 19:9-12; Job 42:6 for some instances.) Many churches use ashes to draw a cross on the forehead of believers on Ash Wednesday. This mark, or one similar to it, is also mentioned several times in the book of Revelation (see 7:3; 9:4; 14:1).

Today, many Christians attend worship services on Ash Wednesday and mark their foreheads with ashes. Some churches use the ashes collected from burned branches left from the previous year's Palm Sunday celebration.[8] Regardless of where the ashes come from, the practice is intended to remind God's people to begin the Lenten season with a humble spirit.

Palm Sunday

They took palm branches and went out to meet him, shouting,
"Hosanna!"
"Blessed is he who comes in the name of the Lord!"
"Blessed is the King of Israel!" (John 12:13)

Palm Sunday, the week before Easter, marks the beginning of Holy Week and commemorates Jesus' triumphal entry into Jerusalem. The account can be found in each of the four Gospels: Matthew 21:1-11; Mark 11:1-11; Luke 19:28-44 and John 12:12-19. Jesus rode into the city on a donkey as the crowd covered His path with palm branches and praised Him. This was a fulfillment of an Old Testament prophecy found in Zechariah 9:9.

Long before Jesus was born, palm branches were waved in celebration during the Feast of Tabernacles and then used to construct the booths the people lived in during the seven days of the feast (see Leviticus 23:40-43). It is no surprise that Webster's dictionary describes palm branches as symbols of victory and rejoicing.[9]

The practice of distributing palm branches on Palm Sunday can be traced back to the fourth century. Today, many churches still hand out palm leaves (sometimes woven into the shape of a cross) during Palm Sunday worship services. Instead of palm branches, the Greek Orthodox Church passes out branches of bay leaves to the congregation to be used for cooking throughout the year.[10]

Maundy Thursday

It was just before the Passover Feast. Jesus knew that the time had come for him to leave this world and go to the Father. Having loved his own who were in the world, he now showed them the full extent of his love. (John 13:1)

Maundy Thursday is celebrated on the Thursday before Easter Sunday to commemorate the Passover Feast Jesus shared with His disciples on the evening before His arrest and crucifixion.[11] An account of this meal is found in all four Gospels: Matthew 26:17-30; Mark 14:12-26; Luke 22:7-23 and John 13:1-4. This event is commonly referred to as "The Lord's Supper" and is the basis for Holy Communion, which is practiced by most Christians throughout the year.

Christians often celebrate Maundy Thursday with a worship service in which the congregation shares Holy Communion. Some churches have even begun to host a traditional Seder dinner to commemorate the holiday as well as introduce members to the Passover celebration.

Good Friday

About the ninth hour Jesus cried out in a loud voice, "Eloi, Eloi, lama sabachthani?"— which means, "My God, my God, why have you forsaken me?" (Matthew 27:46)

This very solemn holiday, celebrated on the Friday before Easter, commemorates the suffering and crucifixion of Jesus as payment for the sins of humanity. Accounts of Jesus' arrest, trial, suffering and death are found in all four Gospels: Matthew 26:47-27:56; Mark 14:43-15:41; Luke 22:47-23:49 and John 18:1-19:37.

The suffering and death of Jesus were the fulfillment of Old Testament prophecy. The most chilling prophecy of Jesus suffering on the cross can be found in Psalm 22. As difficult as it is to dwell on these accounts of the crucifixion, these truths go to the heart of the Christian faith. It is only through the suffering and death of Jesus Christ, who lived a life without sin, that we can claim righteousness before God and enter heaven.

God made him who had no sin to be sin for us, so that in him we might become the righteousness of God. (2 Corinthians 5:21)

Since the death of Jesus is not considered by most to be a happy event, some scholars believe the original name for Good Friday was "God's Friday." They believe the word *good* in the day's current name is most likely a corruption of the German word *gutt*.[12] Other people disagree and believe that "good" represents the precious gift of Jesus to give up His life for the sins of man. Regardless of the origin of the name, throughout history, the day has been marked by Christians with repentance, fasting and prayer.

Today, a few congregations continue the practice of three-hour services to symbolize the length of time Jesus suffered on the cross before He died. Most, however, hold somber services either in the afternoon or the evening.[13] Many of these services are built around Jesus' words from the cross found in the Gospels:

- "My God, my God, why have you forsaken me?" (Matthew 27:46; Mark 15:34)
- "Father, forgive them, for they do not know what they are doing." (Luke 23:34)
- To the thief on the cross: "I tell you the truth, today you will be with me in paradise." (Luke 23:43)
- "Father, into your hands I commit my spirit." (Luke 23:46)
- To His mother, Mary, and His disciple, John, standing at the foot of cross, "'Dear woman, here is your son,' and to the disciple, 'Here is your mother.'" (John 19:26-27)
- "I am thirsty." (John 19:28)
- "It is finished." (John 19:30)

These powerful words have helped believers through the ages understand the great love of God who gave up His life for our sins.

Holy Saturday/Easter Vigil

The traditions surrounding the day before Easter Sunday reach back to the very beginnings of the Christian Church. It was on this day that new believers were received into the Church through Holy Baptism.

Whoever believes and is baptized will be saved. (Mark 16:16)

During this ancient service, which is still practiced in many churches today, the congregation would hold a solemn vigil in anticipation of Jesus' resurrection. The lights in the church would be extinguished and, at midnight, one candle would be lit to represent the risen Christ. This flame would be passed through the congregation to light a candle held by each of the people attending to represent the spread of Jesus' light. The service would end in the joyous proclamation of "He is risen! He is risen indeed!"[14]

For you were once darkness, but now you are light in the Lord. Live as children of light. (Ephesians 5:8)

Easter

The angel said to the women, "Do not be afraid, for I know that you are looking for Jesus, who was crucified. He is not here; he has risen, just as he said." (Matthew 28:5-6)

From that very first morning when the women discovered the empty tomb, Easter (or, as some have come to call it, "Resurrection Day") has been a joyous celebration. All four Gospels contain accounts of this amazing day: Matthew 28:1-10; Mark 16:1-8; Luke 24:1-12 and John 20:1-18.

Jesus' resurrection is the final piece needed to fulfill the prophecy concerning the Messiah who came to save His people. Jesus is the Passover Lamb, sacrificed for the sins of the world.

For you know that it was not with perishable things such as silver or gold that you were redeemed from the empty way of life handed down to you from your forefathers, but with the precious blood of Christ, a lamb without blemish or defect. He was chosen before the creation of the world, but was revealed in these last times for your sake. Through him you believe in God, who raised him from the dead and glorified him, and so your faith and hope are in God. (1 Peter 1:18-21)

Since the Resurrection is so closely associated with the Jewish Passover, the early Church celebrated it at the same time. The early believers, many of them Jewish, considered Jesus' resurrection a new aspect of the Passover celebration. This practice disturbed some factions in the Church because Passover is a moveable feast that does not always fall on a Sunday, and some felt that the Resurrection should always be celebrated on Sunday. In AD 525 the Council of Nicea decreed that the celebration of Christ's resurrection, which by that point had come to be known as Easter, would be celebrated each year on the Sunday following the first full moon after March 21, which is the first day of spring.[15]

Throughout history, Easter has been a day for celebration and feasting. New believers in the early Church developed the practice of wearing white for a full week after Easter Sunday to symbolize light, purity and joy.[16] Today, as in the past, churches are often filled to overflowing as people celebrate the most important truth of the Christian faith: the resurrection of Jesus Christ and His victory over death!

If Christ has not been raised, your faith is futile; you are still in your sins. . . . If only for this life we have hope in Christ, we are to be pitied more than all men.
But Christ has indeed been raised from the dead. (1 Corinthians 15:17, 19-20)

A Closer Look

Test everything. Hold on to the good. (1 Thessalonians 5:21)

All right, all right! So what about the Easter Bunny and colored eggs? As with many holidays, some of the aspects of the culture have been mixed into the celebration. Hold on to your Easter bonnets for this next section.

Scholars say the name "Easter" actually came from "Eostre" which is the name of an Anglo-Saxon goddess of the dawn. Sacrifices were offered to this goddess in the spring, around the same time as Passover. In fact, eggs were rolled along the ground to encourage fertile soil. Many believe that rabbits became associated with the holiday because of a legend where Eostre turned her pet bird into a rabbit because she was angry. (It's beyond me how this tale could end up with a jolly bunny delivering eggs and candy to children.)

Knowing this, what are we, as Christians, to do? Boycott Easter? Egg the Easter Bunny? Frankly, I'm not sure, and I'm certainly not going to try to tell you what to do in your family. (I don't think my computer has enough memory to download all the e-mails I would receive—regardless of which side I came down on this subject.) But, at great personal risk, I *will* pass along a little food for thought. And remember, it's not from me, but from the Apostle Paul.

Though I am free and belong to no man, I make myself a slave to everyone, to win as many as possible. To the Jews I became like a Jew, to win the Jews. To those under the law I became like one under the law (though I myself am not under the law), so as to win those under the law. To those not having the law I became like one not having the law (though I am not free from God's law but am under Christ's law), so as to win those not having the law. To the weak I became weak, to win the weak. I have become all things to all men so that by all possible means I might save some. I do all this for the sake of the gospel, that I may share in its blessings. (1 Corinthians 9:19-23)

Let me tell you what Paul's words mean practically when it comes to *our* family's Easter celebration. Personally, I don't have a problem using the word *Easter*, because if I tried to change the name, most people wouldn't have a clue what I was talking about, and I don't think the gospel would be served by trying to explain it. Take this hypothetical conversation with a neighbor as an example:

"Would you like to join us for Resurrection Sunday dinner?" I ask.
"Sure, when's that?" replies my neighbor.
"The Sunday after next," I say.
"Isn't that Easter Sunday?" she asks.
"Well, yes," I reply, "but we don't use the word *Easter* anymore because it's the name of a pagan goddess who turned her pet bird into a rabbit."
"Oh," says my neighbor. "You know, I think we're busy that day."

Although I am not pushing to purge the word *Easter* from the language, I personally don't care for all the eggs and bunnies everywhere I look. Unless I shop exclusively at the Christian bookstore, I have to search high and low to find anything having to do with the true meaning of the holiday.

What we've done in our family is replace bunnies with lambs (which in my opinion are much cuter and don't bite—at least I don't I think they do). This doesn't mean that I will refuse to visit a home with a bunny on the door, but it does mean that we don't have a bunny flag decorating our porch. Instead, we fly a flag with a butterfly that says, "Forgiven" during the Easter season. (I love when people ask what I need to be forgiven for. "Let me tell you. . . .") Also, we still color eggs, but we decorate them with Christian symbols. We also talk about how eggs represent new life and how we are made new through Jesus Christ. That's what Easter's all about, isn't it?

To sum things up, I have no answer for you. I think the celebration of this most holy day is very personal. Just as we have to come before God and make the very personal decision of whether to accept or reject His offer of eternal life through Jesus Christ, we must do the same with our actions and practices. My prayer is that you will open your heart and allow God to speak to you and that you'll have a *joyous* celebration!

Why do you look for the living among the dead? He is not here; he has risen!

(Luke 24:5-6)

Table Talk

- What about our celebration of the Easter holidays helps us to keep the focus on Jesus? What turns our attention away from Jesus? What do we need to change about the way we celebrate?
- *Ash Wednesday:* Ashes are a symbol of humility and repentance. What do you think it means to humble ourselves before God? Why is this important? What does true repentance mean? How is this shown in our own lives? Personal question: What do you need to repent of this Easter season?
- *Lent:* What will you do to remember Jesus' sacrifice for you during this Lenten season?
- *Palm Sunday:* Palm Sunday is a celebration of praise and acknowledgment of God's victory. In what ways do we praise God? How do we acknowledge Him as King in our lives? What victories have you seen in your own life and in the lives of others?
- *Maundy Thursday:* Why do you think it was necessary for Jesus to give up His body and blood for us? What does it mean when we take Holy Communion? Why is it important for Christians to take part in Holy Communion on a regular basis?
- *Good Friday:* Is this a "good" day for Christians? Why or why not? Why do you think Jesus was willing to suffer so much for us? Would you die a painful and humiliating death for another person? What does it mean to be "crucified with Christ," as it says in Galatians 2:20?
- *Holy Saturday/Easter Vigil:* Jesus is the "light of the world" (John 8:12) and believers are told to pass on this "light." Are you passing on the light of Jesus that is in you? In what way? Is there anything you can do to make your light shine brighter? What does it mean to be the salt and light of the world (see Matthew 5:13-16)?
- *Easter Sunday:* "He has risen!" Read Romans 6:1-14. What does Jesus' resurrection mean in our lives? Does this come with any responsibilities?

Celebrate!

Preschool and Above

- Plant some spring bulbs in a pretty container at the start of Lent. By Easter, you should have a beautiful display of flowers and a great object lesson about how we were once dead in our sins but are now alive through Christ.
- Plant some grass seed in a container with potting soil. In a week or two, you should have a beautiful, natural bed for your colored eggs. By the way, a hardboiled egg, with its three parts, can be a great way to explain the Trinity to children.

Elementary and Above

- Attend a traditional Seder dinner sponsored by a Messianic Jewish congregation. The Passover Seder commemorates the deliverance of the Jewish people from slavery in Egypt. It was through the Seder dinner that Jesus ate with His disciples the night before He was arrested that He was able to communicate God's plan of redemption. We have found that celebrating this special dinner with Jewish believers in Jesus is one of the most meaningful parts of our Easter celebration. If you can't find a Messianic congregation in your area, pick up a copy of a book on the Passover Haggadah at your Christian bookstore and host your own.

- Learn to share the gospel using jelly beans and commit to sharing it this Easter season with someone who may not know the good news. You just need four jelly beans (black, red, white, green). Give the person the jelly beans one at a time and say:
  - "This black jelly bean represents our hearts without God. It is black with sin."
  - "This red jelly bean represents the blood of Jesus, who gave His life to pay the penalty of our sin."
  - "When we admit our sin and accept our need for God, our hearts become clean. That's why I have this white jelly bean. There is nothing we can do to wash away our sin. Jesus' death on the cross was full payment."
  - "The green jelly bean represents eternal life. Eternal life means that if a person died right this minute, he or she would go to heaven. Eternal life is the gift God is offering us if we will just trust in Him."
  - "Have you accepted this gift? If you were to die tonight, are you sure you would be in heaven? If not, would you like to pray with me right now and accept Jesus as your Savior?"

    (If so, help the person pray by having him repeat the words after you.) "Dear Jesus, I admit that I have sinned and am not worthy to be called Your child or to enter heaven. There is nothing I can do to make myself worthy in Your sight. I believe that You paid the penalty for my sins by dying on the cross. I am sorry for my sins and ask for Your forgiveness. I also ask that You help me live a life that allows me to be worthy of being called Your child. I love You, Lord. Amen."

Teenager and Above

- Instead of giving up a certain food or activity during the Lenten season, consider giving up some of your time. Help out at a charity or do some community service. Join a Bible study or commit to spending a certain amount of time each day in prayer or reading the Bible.

- Make a Lamb cake for your Easter celebration. This Easter tradition has been passed down through the Salzmann family for several generations. Even this domestically challenged in-law is able to pull off this dessert. You can find a lamb cake mold and instructions at a craft store in the cake decorating section.

Recipes to Enjoy

Easter Breakfast

My friend Rosemary taught me how to make this wonderful and wonderfully easy Easter breakfast!

Just buy a bag of frozen sweet rolls (the kind that need to rise as they thaw). Spray a 13 x 9-inch glass pan with cooking oil. Place the rolls in the pan and tuck uncooked colored eggs in between the rolls. Cover and place in the refrigerator for 12-14 hours. As the dough thaws, it will rise around the eggs. Bake everything according to the sweet roll package directions (yes, even the eggs) in the morning. Frost the rolls and sprinkle them with pastel decorating "sprinkles" (or whatever they are called). Your eggs will be soft-cooked and will be a perfect accompaniment to your sweet rolls!

Hot Cross Buns

These tasty treats are a traditional Lenten favorite! I streamline the process by using a bread machine to make the dough.

Place ingredients in a 1 1/2 lb. bread machine in the following order:

1 1/3 cups warm milk
2 eggs
2 T. butter
4 cups flour
3 T. sugar
1 t. salt
1/2 t. cinnamon
1/4 t. nutmeg
2 t. active dry yeast

Run the bread machine on the dough cycle. During the last minute or so of mixing, add 3/4 cup raisins.

When the cycle is complete, remove the dough from the machine to a floured surface. Punch the dough down and let it rest for 10 minutes. Then, divide the dough into 24 portions and shape into smooth balls. Place in rows on greased baking sheets 1 1/2 inches apart. Cover and let rise until they are almost double in size (for about an hour). Bake in a 375°F oven for 15 minutes until golden brown. Make a cross on each bun with powdered sugar frosting.

To make frosting: Mix 1/2 cup powdered sugar, 1/4 t. vanilla and milk to make desired consistency.

Easter Story Cookie

My friend Boots gave me this fun idea to share the Easter story with children. You even end up with a delicious treat in the morning!

You'll need:
  1 cup whole pecans
  1 t. vinegar
  3 egg whites
  Pinch of salt
  1 cup sugar
  Zipper baggie
  Wooden spoons
  Duct tape
  Bible

Preheat oven to 300°F. Place pecans in zipper baggie. Let children beat the pecans with a wooden spoon to break the pecans into small pieces. Explain that Jesus was beaten by soldiers when He was arrested.

Let each child smell the vinegar before putting it in the mixing bowl. Explain that when Jesus was thirsty on the cross, He was given vinegar to drink.

Add egg whites to the vinegar. Explain that eggs represent life and that Jesus gave His life to give us eternal life.

Sprinkle a little salt in each child's hand. Let them taste it, then have them brush the rest into the bowl. Explain that this represents the salty tears shed by Jesus' followers and also the bitterness of sin.

So far, the ingredients haven't been very appetizing. Add one cup of sugar. Explain that the sweetest part of the story is that Jesus died because He loves us. He wants us to belong to Him.

Beat the ingredients with a mixer on high speed for 12-15 minutes until stiff peaks form. Explain that the color white represents the purity in God's eyes of those whose sins have been cleansed by Jesus.

Fold broken nuts into the egg mixture. Drop by teaspoons onto a cookie sheet covered with waxed paper. Explain that each mound represents the rocky tomb where Jesus was laid.

Put the cookie sheet in the oven, close the door and turn the oven off. Give each child a piece of duct tape and have them seal the oven door. Explain that Jesus' tomb was sealed.

Go to bed. Explain that just as they may feel sad to leave the cookies in the oven overnight, Jesus' followers were also very sad when His tomb was sealed.

On Easter morning, open the oven and give everyone a cookie. Notice the cracks on top. Take a bite and see that the cookies are hollow. On the first Easter, Jesus' followers were amazed to find His tomb open and empty! He has risen!

Notes

1. US Embassy Public Affairs, "Celebrate! Holidays in the USA" [on-line], August 16, 2002. Available from: <http://www.usembassy.de/usa/etexts/hol/celebrate.pdf>.
2. Ibid.
3. Ibid.
4. Ibid.
5. Bernard Ramm, "Lent," *The World Book Encyclopedia* (Chicago, IL: Field Enterprises Educational Corporation, 1969), p. L-175.
6. James Akin, "Ash Wednesday" [on-line], January 22, 2004. Available from: <http://www.cin.org/users/james/files/ash_wed.htm>.
7. "Origin and History of Ash Wednesday" [on-line], August 10, 2002. Available from: <http://www.theholidayspot.com/ash_wednesday/origin.htm>.
8. Akin.
9. "Palm," *Merriam Webster's Collegiate Dictionary Tenth Edition* (Springfield, MA: Merriam-Webster, Inc., 1996), p. 837.
10. "Annie's Palm Sunday Page" [on-line], August 10, 2002. Available from: <http://www.annieshomepage.com/palm-sunday.html>.
11. "Maundy Thursday" [on-line], August 10, 2002. Available from: <http://www.factmonster.com/ce6/society/A0832274.html>.
12. Chris Armstrong, "The Goodness of Good Friday" [on-line], April 17, 2002. *Christianity Today*, January 22, 2004. Available from: <http://www.christianitytoday.com/ct/2003/115/44.0.html>.
13. The Columbia Electronic Encyclopedia on Fact Monster, "Good Friday" [on-line], August 10, 2002. Available from: <http://www.factmonster.com/ce6/society/A0821267.html>.
14. "Annie's Easter History Page" [on-line], August 10, 2002. Available from: <http://www.annieshomepage.com/easter-history.html>.
15. Ibid.
16. Ibid.

 # May

Hebrew: **Ziv** (see 1 Kings 6:1)

Mother's Day
2nd Sunday in May

Memorial Day
Last Monday in May

The whole assembly then agreed to **celebrate***.*
(2 Chronicles 30:23)

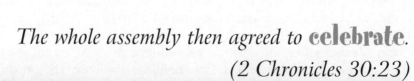

Key Verse

May she who gave you birth rejoice! (Proverbs 23:25)

A Little History

No man is poor who has a godly mother.
        —Abraham Lincoln[1]

Dirty diapers, scraped knees, soccer games, peanut butter sandwiches and count-less loads of laundry. At least once a year, the challenges of everyday life are for-gotten as children in the United States take time out to let their mothers know how much they appreciate them.

The idea of setting aside a day to recognize mothers is not unique to the United States. England was one of the first countries to establish what came to be known as "Mothering Sunday." In the eighteenth century, when many people worked as house-hold servants for the rich, the fourth Sunday after Lent was reserved for them to go home to be with their mothers. Though this custom stopped when the Industrial Revo-lution changed the working and living patterns of the people, a "Sunday for Mothers" was established as a holiday in the early 1900s.[2]

The love and perseverance of one grateful daughter, Anna Jarvis, is credited with help-ing to establish Mother's Day in the United States. Anna's mother had worked very hard throughout her life to establish "Mother's Friendship Day" in an attempt to heal the scars of the Civil War. Moved by her mother's dedication to this cause, Anna held a service in Grafton, West Virginia, two years after her month's death to honor her. Anna was so touched by the ceremony that she began a letter-writing campaign to adopt a formal holiday to honor mothers. In 1910, the governor of West Virginia proclaimed the second Sunday in May as Mother's Day and, a year later, every state celebrated the holiday.[3] In 1914, President Woodrow Wilson made it official and proclaimed Mother's Day as "a public expression of love and reverence for the mothers of our country."[4]

On Mother's Day morning, some American children follow the tradition of serving their mothers breakfast in bed. Other children will give their mothers gifts that they have made themselves or bought in stores. Adults may give their mothers red carnations, the official Mother's Day flower. If their mothers have died, they may bring white carnations to their grave sites.[5] This is also the busiest day of the year for American restaurants, as families give Mom a day off from the kitchen![6]

A Closer Look

Sons are a heritage from the LORD,
*   children a reward from him. (Psalm 127:3)*

Just as children are precious blessings to mothers, mothers are blessings to their children. With the blessings come responsibilities on both sides. The Bible tells us that children are to:

"Honor your father and mother"—which is the first commandment with a promise—"that it may go well with you and that you may enjoy long life on the earth." (Ephesians 6:2-3)

Webster's dictionary defines *honor* (in the verb form) as "to regard or treat with great respect."[7] What does this mean practically? It's a difficult question, because all mothers and all situations are different.

Some children, particularly adults who may carry wounds from childhood, may find it difficult to respect their parents. However, it's important to note that God does not say that we are to honor our parents because of their behavior, but that we are to honor them because of the position they hold. Even when it's difficult, God promises that our obedience to this command will bring His blessing to our lives.

We can honor our mothers by:

- diligently praying for them
- taking the opportunity to offer honest affirmation and encouragement
- cultivating thoughtfulness through regular visits, thank-you notes and letters or e-mails
- being available to offer help (both practical, emotional and, if necessary, financial) when needed, while at the same time respecting their rights to make their own decisions
- doing what is in our power to maintain harmony among siblings and other family members
- teaching our children to do the same

While the attention and appreciation given to mothers on Mother's Day is wonderful and appropriate, it also gives a mother an opportunity to see what a powerful impact she has on the lives of the children with which God has entrusted her. The Bible provides us with a wonderful example of a godly mother in the description of the woman in Proverbs 31:

She speaks with wisdom,
*   and faithful instruction is on her tongue.*
She watches over the affairs of her household
*   and does not eat the bread of idleness.*
Her children arise and call her blessed;
*   her husband also, and he praises her.*
*   (Proverbs 31:26-28)*

Before we talk about what these verses mean to mothers, I need to tell you not expect to be called "blessed" by your children any time during the teen years, unless you are handing over money or the car keys. Also, I'm not sure teenagers even know the definition of the word *arise*.

Now, what does this shining example of motherhood mean practically? Frankly, it scares me out of my wits! (Especially the part about wisdom and faithful instruction on my tongue.) I do know that because God has given me the blessing of children, He has called me to motherhood. I have also heard it said by many Christian leaders that God does not call the equipped, but He equips the called. My responsibility is to stay closely connected to God, which means that I need to spend a lot of time on my knees.

> *I am the Vine; you are the branches. Whoever lives in Me and I in him bears much (abundant) fruit. However, apart from Me [cut off from vital union with Me] you can do nothing. (John 15:5, Amp.)*

So what do mothers get out of all this fruit bearing? Just listen:

> *Charm is deceptive, and beauty is*
> *   fleeting;*
> *but a woman who fears the LORD is*
> *   to be praised.*
> *Give her the reward she has earned,*
> *   and let her works bring her praise at*
> *   the city gate.*
> *   (Proverbs 31:30-31)*

Table Talk

- What do you appreciate most about your mom?
- What are some of the special blessings you have received by being a mom?
- What does it mean to "honor" another person? What are some things that can get in the way of doing this?

Celebrate!

Preschool and Above

Flowers are a traditional expression of love and affection on Mother's Day. Although the carnation is the "official" Mother's Day flower, a bouquet of mom's favorite posies, even from the backyard (wait, I better qualify this one: Before going out and picking all of the new blooms off of Mom's prize rose bush, little ones should definitely check with an adult) is always a welcome treat!

- Children can make a precious memory for Mom or Grandma that she can use every day. Decorate plain, white ceramic dishes (plates, bowls or mugs are great) with special paint made for dishes. You can find this paint at most craft or art supply stores. My friend, Sarah, suggests helping small children put their handprints on a plate. Each Mother's Day, add another dish to the collection with an updated handprint or drawing.

Elementary and Above

- Mothers just love it when their kids surprise them with breakfast in bed or perhaps a picnic at a favorite spot.
- In nineteenth-century England, the children would take over the chores on "Mothering Sunday" so their mothers could go to church. Thoughtful children could continue this custom today by presenting their mothers with "coupons" redeemable for household chores. For example: "This entitles Mom to one hour of my time to do the household chores of her choice. Love, Freddy." Moms with young children or elderly mothers might also appreciate the services of a professional housekeeper for a day. (What am I saying?! Mothers of any age or stage would *love* this gift!)

Teenagers and Above

- Put together a "theme" basket full of small gifts your mother might like such as: luxury bath items, cooking gadgets and a cookbook, scrapbooking supplies, movie or video store gift certificates with popcorn and candy, gardening supplies with a "coupon" for weed-pulling services, etc. The possibilities are endless!
- Another custom from England is for the oldest son to take his mother a "Mothering Cake" on this special day. For years, my son Freddy has made me my favorite chocolate sour cream cake with raspberries and whipped cream. Now that's "mothering"!
- Do you know a mother who lives alone—or perhaps a single mother with small children? What can you do to make her day special?

Recipes to Enjoy

Mother's Day Roast

   3 lb. beef roast (any kind except brisket)
   1 can cream of mushroom soup
   1 envelope dry onion soup mix
   1 16-ounce package baby carrots
   3-4 potatoes, scrubbed and cut in chunks

Put roast in crock pot. Top with onion and mushroom soups. Add carrots and potatoes. Cover and cook on low for 8-10 hours or on high for 5-6 hours. (Do not add liquid. The soups combine with the meat juices to make a wonderful sauce—trust me.)

"Luv You SOOO Much" Fruit Salad

1 15-ounce can chunky fruit cocktail, undrained
1 15-ounce can pineapple tidbits, undrained
1 11-ounce can mandarin oranges, drained
1 3-ounce box instant vanilla pudding
1 cup whipped topping

Mix together. Refrigerate for at least an hour before serving.

"I Made It Myself" Tropical Pie

1 vanilla cookie crust (or may substitute graham cracker crust)
1 16-ounce can crushed pineapple, undrained
1 3-ounce box vanilla instant pudding
1 cup sour cream
Whipped topping

Mix the pineapple, pudding and sour cream together. Put into the crust. Chill for 2-4 hours. Top with whipped topping when served. (My friend Rosemary also garnishes each slice with a little toasted coconut and a maraschino cherry!)

Memorial Day
Last Monday in May

Key Verse

Nor should the memory of them die out among their descendants. (Esther 9:28)

A Little History

I will perpetuate your memory through all generations. (Psalm 45:17)

As with many holidays, there is much disagreement about the birthplace of Memorial Day, or Decoration Day, as it was originally called. In fact, up to twenty-four communities, from Waterloo, New York, to Carbondale, Illinois, claim to have held the first Memorial Day celebration.[8] The good news, at least for those interested in the origins of holidays, is that there is widespread agreement about *why* it was established. Memorial Day was conceived as a way of remembrance and healing from the long and bloody Civil War.[9]

The "official" birthplace of Memorial Day is Waterloo, New York, per a declaration by President Lyndon Johnson on the holiday's 100-year anniversary.[10] It's said that Henry Welles, a local merchant, so moved by the tales of soldiers returning from the Civil War, suggested that all the shops in town close for one day to honor those who were killed. On the morning of May 5, 1866, townspeople decorated the graves of the Civil War veterans with flowers, crosses and flags.[11]

A retired officer, Major General Jonathan Logan, planned a separate ceremony involving those who had survived the war. In 1868, the two ceremonies were joined and General Logan officially proclaimed the purpose of the holiday as an opportunity to

> gather around their sacred remains and garland the passionless mounds above them with choicest flowers of springtime. . . . Let us in this solemn presence renew our pledges to aid and assist those whom they have left among us as sacred charges upon the Nation's gratitude, the soldier's and sailor's widow and orphan.[12]

The South refused to acknowledge the day, honoring their dead on separate days until after World War I, when the holiday changed from honoring just those who died fighting in the Civil War to honoring Americans who died fighting in any war.[13] In 1971, along with other holidays, President Richard Nixon declared Memorial Day a federal holiday to be celebrated on the last Monday in May.[14]

Today, Memorial Day is not limited to a day of remembrance for military veterans. It has also become a time to remember family members who have died. Individuals and families honor loved ones by attending church services and decorating grave sites with flowers. For many Americans, the three-day Memorial Day weekend also signals the beginning of summer, which is often celebrated with barbecues, picnics and other outdoor gatherings.

In Waterloo, New York, the original purpose of Memorial Day is scrupulously preserved. Every May 30, townspeople walk to the cemeteries, decorate the graves of veterans with flags and flowers and hold a memorial service. Citizens then walk back to the park in the middle of town where two historic documents are read: General Logan's Order #11, originally designating Decoration Day as an observed holiday, and President Lincoln's Gettysburg Address.[15]

> From these honored dead, we take increased devotion to that cause for which they here gave the last full measure of devotion—that we here highly resolve these dead shall not have died in vain.
>
> —Abraham Lincoln, Gettysburg Address[16]

A Closer Look

The memory of the righteous will be a blessing. (Proverbs 10:7)

A *memorial* is defined by Webster's dictionary as "something that keeps a memory alive."[17] How are you keeping your special memories alive? I have yet to meet a person who doesn't struggle with what to keep and what to throw out. For me, there's no easy answer. It always seems that what is trash to me is treasure to another family member.

As I struggled with this dilemma year after year, it finally occurred to me that the real question wasn't so much what to keep, but what to leave behind. What do I want others to remember about me and about our family? What will be our legacy to future generations?

As I thought about these questions, it became very easy to toss the collection of party favors I had collected in college as well as the spelling tests from my daughter's third grade year. I finally came to realize that the real blessing to my children, and to my children's children, is a spiritual legacy.

About now you may be thinking, "Sounds great—on paper. But I still have eight years of vacation photos to organize!" All I can say is, "So do I, but please keep reading."

Frankly, as I looked at my boxes, bags and piles of "memories," I was tempted to just cart it all out to the curb for the trash haulers. After all, what spiritual truths will future generations glean from our vacation photos at the beach? But before I could get the wheelbarrow, I began to think about those stacks of paper and photos in a new way. I began to think of them as steps along a path, one that was directed and ordained by God. In one of those rare "light-bulb moments," I realized I had all the makings to record a powerful spiritual journey for future generations, and so do you!

How do we do this? There are lots of ways, but I believe the first step is prayer. Ask God what He would like you to leave to future generations about how He has worked in your life and in the life of your family. Also ask for the grace to let go of pride and provide a genuine account of your journey in a way that suits how God uniquely made you.

The following are some ideas I've gleaned from friends, observation and personal experience. Perhaps one will appeal to you.

- As you scrapbook photos or assemble family memories, record the spiritual blessings and lessons connected with the events. For example, while visiting Mayan ruins in Mexico on one vacation, I learned much more about evil than I did about architecture. When I get a chance to put the photos from the trip into a scrapbook or album, I will be sure to write down the lessons I learned.

- Pass along a well-used Bible. On my son Freddy's confirmation of faith, I presented him with my Bible. It was the Bible I had used for the previous eight years while enrolled in Bible Study Fellowship. Through this rather intensive program, I had studied most books of the Bible, and as God opened my eyes to the truth of His Word, I underlined passages and made many notes in the margins. Often, I would also jot down comments like, "Lord, I'm not sure I understand this." I felt that my struggle to understand God's Word would be a blessing to Freddy *now*, not when I was gone.

  I'll be honest with you, letting go of my Bible—even to my son—was a struggle for me. I hated to give up this record of God's work in my life. I admitted this to a friend one day, concerned that I might be making the Bible an "idol." She responded by saying, "Oh, Cyndy, just think of all the new things God has to teach you as you study in a brand new Bible!" Her words touched my heart, giving me new resolve to pass this treasured possession to my son and helping me to look forward to the new truth God would open up to me in His Word. Giving up my well-worn Bible was a way to pass along a spiritual legacy to my son and, maybe someday, to his son.

- Archive your prayer journals. I have been writing my prayers in a journal for many years. I keep the journals in envelopes (marked by year) in the back of my closet. These journals are letters to God in which I open up my heart with no intention for others to read what I've written. If I were "constructing" a journal for posterity, my words probably wouldn't be honest. Right now, I'm not sure if I will pass these journals along or destroy them. I'm trusting God for the wisdom to make that decision when the time is right.

- Pass along a favorite book or devotional. Include a note in the front of the book explaining what you learned from the book or how God has used it to impact your life.

  Although I had heard much about Oswald Chambers' *My Utmost for His Highest*, I didn't take the time to explore it until a close friend of my husband passed along his copy to us. He said that he and his wife had learned much from Chambers' words and they thought we might like it. His words piqued my interest. The book is now a daily favorite that I hope my husband and I have an opportunity to share with someone else.

- Write down your testimony. Record how you came to know Jesus and accept Him as your Lord and Savior. It doesn't have to be a dramatic story. Just write from your heart.

  The key isn't *how* you pass along a spiritual legacy, it's being intentional about doing it. Don't fret about passing along great spiritual insight or a perfect walk with God.

I've been encouraged the most by learning about the struggles of others, people like Abraham, David, Peter and even Jesus. So leave a record of your spiritual victories *and* your struggles. Allow future generations a peek into the heart of a *real* person who loves God.

Table Talk

- Share a special memory about an individual or family member who has died.
- How can remembering someone who has died help in the healing process?
- How would you like to be remembered? What would cause people to remember you in this way?
- What can you do to honor those who have died serving our country in the armed forces? Why is this important?

Celebrate!

Preschool and Above

- Make a thank-you card for someone you know who is serving or has served in the military.
- Put up a flag and fly it at half-mast to remember those who have sacrificed their lives for their country. This may also provide an opportunity to talk about our hope for eternal life through Jesus.

Elementary Age and Above

- Sample some "hardtack" (see recipe on the next page). This was a hard bread eaten by soldiers during the Civil War. It was stored in large barrels that often became infested with bugs. At times it was the only food available to the troops. In fact, one soldier wrote in his journal, "The only fresh meat we had came in the barrels of bread."[18] Yuck! See what you think of "hardtack," but please leave out the bugs!
- Join the rest of the nation and take part in a moment of silence at 3 p.m. on Memorial Day. Use this time to pray for the needs of our leaders and armed forces.

Teens and Above

- Visit a war memorial or military cemetery. Try to attend the Memorial Day celebration. Take time to thank those veterans who attend the ceremony for their service to our country.
- If your extended family gets together for a Memorial Day picnic or barbecue, take the opportunity to ask them about their lives, memories, etc. It would be great if you could audio- or videotape their answers.

- Take some time to write out your testimony. How did you come to know Jesus? What difference has this made in your life?

Recipes to Enjoy

Hardtack

2 cups flour
1 cup water
1 T. shortening or lard
1/2 t. salt

Mix all ingredients and roll out dough in a 1/2-inch-thick square or rectangle. Bake for 30 minutes at 400°F. Remove from oven. While warm, cut dough into 3-inch squares and punch four rows of holes into each square. Turn dough over, return to the oven and bake another 30 minutes.

For those of us who live away from family members, a three-day weekend offers an opportunity to travel back "home" for a family barbecue. Here are a few of the recipes we can always count on when the Salzmann clan gathers for Memorial Day.

Aunt Shirley's Coleslaw

1 cup chopped celery
1 green pepper, chopped
2 t. salt
1 t. celery seed
1/2 t. mustard seed
3/4 cup sugar
3/4 cup vinegar
2 T. salad oil
1 medium head cabbage

Shred cabbage. Add other ingredients. Allow to sit several hours before serving.

Potato Gooey

1 24-ounce package of frozen hash browns
1 can cream of mushroom soup (or any cream soup)
1 cup sour cream
2 cups grated cheddar cheese
1/2 cup chopped onion

Mix ingredients and put into a greased 13 x 9 x 2-inch baking dish. Bake at 350°F for about one hour.

If you would like a topping, mix:

1 1/2 cups crushed corn flakes or bread crumbs
1/4 cup melted butter

Sprinkle on top before baking.

Chris's Barbecue Ribs

Marinate desired amount of country-style ribs in bottled Italian salad dressing overnight. Barbecue ribs over very low heat on grill, basting with marinade for at least two hours. During the last 30 minutes, baste the ribs with barbecue sauce, if desired. (I realize this recipe is a bit vague, but it's from a man. They always come out really well, so just roll with it and see what happens.)

Mother's Coconut Cake

6 eggs
1 cup shortening
1/2 cup butter
3 cups sugar
1/2 t. almond extract
1/2 t. coconut extract
3 cups cake flour
1 t. salt
1 cup milk
2 cups coconut, shredded or flaked

Separate eggs into large bowls and allow whites to come to room temperature. Meanwhile, preheat oven to 300°F. Grease a 10-inch tube or bundt pan well. (Note: This recipe makes too much batter for one pan. You will have enough to make another small cake in a loaf pan.)

Beat egg yolks with shortening and butter. Gradually add sugar, beating until light and fluffy. Add extracts. Mix salt with flour. Add flour to mixture alternately with milk, beginning and ending with flour. Stir in coconut.

Beat egg whites until soft peaks form. Gently fold whites into batter until well combined. Put in pan.

Bake for two hours or until a cake tester inserted in the center comes out clean. Cool on a wire rack for 10 minutes. Remove from pan. When cool, dust with powdered sugar.

Notes

1. Roy B. Zuck, *The Speaker's Quote Book* (Grand Rapids, MI: Kregel Publications, 1997), p. 263.
2. US Embassy Public Affairs, "Celebrate! Holidays in the USA" [on-line], August 16, 2002. Available from: <http://www.usembassy.de/usa/etexts/hol/celebrate.pdf>.
3. "Everything Mothers Day: History of Mother's Day" [on-line], August 16, 2002. Available from: <http://www.everythingmothersday.com/news/history.asp>.
4. Ibid.

5. US Embassy Public Affairs.

6. Ibid.

7. "Honor," *Merriam Webster's Collegiate Dictionary Tenth Edition* (Springfield, MA: Merriam-Webster, Inc., 1996), p. 557.

8. "Memorial Day History" [on-line], August 16, 2002. Available from: <http://www.usmemorialday.org/backgrnd.html>.

9. Ibid.

10. US Embassy Public Affairs.

11. Ibid.

12. Ibid.

13. "Memorial Day History."

14. Ibid.

15. US Embassy Public Affairs.

16. "Gettysburg Address" [on-line], May 8, 2004. Available from: <http://www.quoteworld.org/docs/alget328.php>.

17. "Memorial," *Merriam Webster's Collegiate Dictionary Tenth Edition* (Springfield, MA: Merriam-Webster, Inc., 1996), p. 725.

18. Office of Historic Alexandria, "What Is Hardtack?" [on-line], August 16, 2002. Available from: <http://www.geocities.com/Pentagon/Barracks/1369/recipes.html>

June

Hebrew: **Sivan** (see Esther 8:9)

Flag Day
June 14

Father's Day
3rd Sunday in June

They will **celebrate** *your abundant goodness.*

(Psalm 145:7)

Flag Day

June 14

Key Verse

We . . . will lift up our banners in the name of our God. (Psalm 20:5)

A Little History

One nation under God.

—United States Pledge of Allegiance

The inspiration for Flag Day is credited to Wisconsin schoolteacher, B.J. Cigland. On the 108th anniversary of the adoption of the Stars and Stripes in 1885, Cigland's students celebrated the first Flag Day. He later continued as an enthusiastic advocate through numerous magazine and newspaper articles as well as public speeches.[1] The idea spread quickly, and soon both adults and children across the nation were commemorating "Old Glory's" birthday. Inspired by thirty years of observance, President Woodrow Wilson officially proclaimed June 14 as Flag Day. It was not until 1949, however, that National Flag Day became a legal holiday through an Act of Congress.[2]

The first flag, known as the Grand Union, was flown at the headquarters of the Continental Army in 1776. Although there is some controversy regarding the origin of the flag, the most widely circulated account is that it was designed by George Washington and sewn by Betsy Ross, a seamstress who made flags for ships. It had thirteen stars in a circle to represent each colony. It's said that Betsy Ross suggested the circle design to signify that no state was greater than the others.[3]

The Flag Act of 1818 stipulates that a new star be added for each new state on the Independence Day following the state's admission to the Union. The current US flag has fifty stars on a blue field with thirteen red and white stripes representing the original thirteen colonies.[4]

The colors used in the flag are also symbolic. White signifies purity and innocence, red hardiness and valor and blue vigilance, perseverance and justice.[5]

Pledge of Allegiance

The Pledge of Allegiance was written by Baptist minister Francis Bellamy to commemorate the 400-year anniversary of Columbus' voyage to America. It was published on September 8, 1892, in *The Youth's Companion*. On October 21, 1892, Reverend Bellamy watched as 6,000 children recited the pledge in Boston. They were joined by thousands of others across the nation, including a large group of both children and adults at the Chicago World's Fair.[6]

In 1942, Congress made the Pledge of Allegiance part of the Federal Flag Code.[7] In 1954, lawmakers added two important words to the Pledge—"under God"—declaring to the world, in the words of President Dwight D. Eisenhower, "the importance of religious faith in America's heritage and future."[8]

In response to a 2002 court case challenging the use of the words "under God" in the Pledge, President George W. Bush signed law S.2690. This law is a reaffirmation of "one nation under God" in the Pledge of Allegiance and "In God We Trust" as the National Motto.[9] As he signed this important bill, the President affirmed that "our nation was built upon faith in God, and these important truths are not subject to trends, popular belief or the special interests of a vocal minority."[10]

> I pledge allegiance to the flag of the United States of America and to the republic for which it stands, one nation, under God, indivisible, with liberty and justice for all.
> —United States Pledge of Allegiance

Flag Etiquette

On Flag Day in 1923, lawmakers approved the Federal Flag Code as a guide for the handling and display of the American Flag.[11] Although no criminal penalties are attached to the law, the Code outlines proper flag etiquette, including the following:

- The flag should only be displayed from sunrise to sunset unless it is illuminated.
- Only all-weather flags should be displayed in inclement weather.
- When displayed on a flagpole, the flag should be raised briskly and lowered ceremoniously.
- Never let the flag touch the ground or drape it over vehicles or other objects. The flag should be allowed to fly free.
- On a staff, no other flag should be placed above the American flag.
- When displayed, the stars should be to the left and the stripes to the right.
- Never use the flag for clothing or decoration. Instead, use bunting with the blue on top, then white, then red.

Star-Spangled Banner

"The Star-Spangled Banner" was written by Francis Scott Key during the War of 1812. Key wrote the verses after a long night of captivity on an enemy ship while the British attacked Fort McHenry. As the cannons fired, Key is said to have prayed fervently through the night for the Americans to hold on. When he saw the Stars and Stripes still waving over the fort in the morning, he knew the American troops had prevailed. Key was so overjoyed that he quickly penned the poem that became America's national anthem in 1931.[12]

Little did Francis Scott Key know that his heartfelt poem would become a song that touches the hearts of Americans each time it is sung or that America's national motto, "In God We Trust," would be drawn from the fourth stanza of his beloved hymn of thanksgiving:

O! thus be it ever when freemen shall stand
    Between their loved homes and the foe's desolation;
Blessed with victory and peace, may our heaven-rescued land
    Praise the Power that hath made and preserved us a nation,
Then conquer we must, for our cause it is just—
    And this be our motto—"In God is our trust!"
"The Star Spangled Banner"[13]

A Closer Look

> We take the stars and blue union from heaven, the red from our mother country, separating it by white stripes, thus showing we have separated from her, and the white stripes shall go down to posterity representing liberty.
>
> —Quote often attributed to George Washington[14]

A flag is much more than a colorful symbol for a nation. It represents a country's values, hopes and dreams, both past and present. It says much about what binds us together as citizens and what separates us from other nations of the world.

The United States was founded by men of deep faith who designed our government according to biblical principles. This was reiterated by US Supreme Court Chief Justice Earl Warren in 1954:

> I believe no one can read the history of our country without realizing that the Good Book and the spirit of the Savior have from the beginning been our guiding geniuses. . . . Whether we look to the first Charter of Virginia . . . or to the Charter of New England . . . the same objective is present . . . a Christian land governed by Christian principles. I believe the entire Bill of Rights came into being because of the knowledge our forefathers had of the Bible and their belief in it: freedom of belief, of expression, of assembly, of petition, the dignity of the individual, the sanctity of the home, equal justice under law, and the reservation of powers to the people.[15]

Our flag stands as a symbol of our heritage as a nation built on the faith of our founding fathers and should be treated with dignity and respect. I have found no place where this is more clearly illustrated than in the flag-folding ceremony practiced at the United States Air Force Academy. The ceremony begins with the following:

> The flag-folding ceremony represents the same religious principles on which our country was originally founded. The portion of the flag denoting honor is the canton of blue containing the stars representing the states our veterans served in uniform. The canton field of blue dresses from left to right and is inverted when draped as a pall on a casket of a veteran who has served our country in uniform.
>
> In the Armed Forces of the United States, at the ceremony of retreat, the flag is lowered, folded in a triangle fold and kept under watch throughout the night as a tribute to our nation's honored dead. The next morning it is brought out and, at the ceremony of reveille, run aloft as a symbol of our belief in the resurrection of the body.[16]

The ceremony contains a detailed account of what each part of the flag represents and what each fold made in the flag stands for. The biblical basis of some of the symbolism in the ceremony is unmistakable, such as:

The first fold of our flag is a symbol of life.
The second fold is a symbol of our belief in the eternal life. . . .
The eighth fold is a tribute to the one who entered in to the valley of the shadow of death, that we might see the light of day, and to honor mother, for whom it flies on Mother's Day. . . .
The twelfth fold, in the eyes of a Christian citizen, represents an emblem of eternity and glorifies, in their eyes, God the Father, the Son, and Holy Ghost.
When the flag is completely folded, the stars are uppermost, reminding us of our national motto, "In God We Trust."[17]

Next time you pledge allegiance to "Old Glory," pause to remember how the faith of our founding fathers, and their allegiance to Almighty God, is intricately woven into each thread of our country's most important national symbol.

Table Talk

- Why is it important for a nation to have a flag?
- In the early 1990s, there was a national movement to amend the US Constitution to make vandalizing the flag by a US citizen a crime. Lawmakers abandoned this legislation because they felt it would limit a citizen's freedom of speech. Do you agree or disagree with this decision? Why?
- Do you think the general moral philosophy of the United States today reflects the symbolism the founding fathers intended when the flag was designed? Why or why not?
- If you had a personal flag, what would you include on it? Why?

Celebrate!

Preschool and Above

- Decorate your yard with American flags in honor of Flag Day.
- Recite the Pledge of Allegiance as a family.
- Eat a red, white and blue meal: spaghetti with red sauce, blue gelatin and a big glass of white milk!

Elementary Age and Above

- Learn how to fold a flag correctly:

1. Begin by holding it waist-high with another person so that its surface is parallel to the ground.

2. Fold the lower half of the striped section lengthwise over the field of stars, holding the bottom and top edges securely.
3. Fold the flag again lengthwise with the blue field on the outside.
4. Make a triangular fold by bringing the striped corner of the folded edge to meet the open (top) edge of the flag.
5. Turn the outer (end) point inward, parallel to the open edge, to form a second triangle.
6. The triangular folding is continued until the entire length of the flag is folded in this manner.
7. When the flag is completely folded, only a triangular blue field of stars should be visible.

Teens and Above

- Design a flag to symbolize your heritage, values and dreams.
- Look up the Federal Flag Code (Public Law 94-344) to learn proper flag etiquette. Why is how we treat the flag important?

Recipes to Enjoy

Old Glory Muffins

A patriotic way to start the day!

Prepare your favorite blueberry muffin recipe or packaged mix. Add 1/2 cup dried cherries or cranberries. Bake as directed. These are best served warm from the oven.

Patriotic Cupcake Cones

These little treats are soooo cute and fun to eat!

Packaged cake mix (any flavor)
White frosting (homemade or canned)
Red, white and blue sprinkles
2 dozen ice-cream cones (flat bottom kind, not sugar style)

Prepare cake mix according to package directions. Stand ice-cream cones in muffin tins and half-fill the cones with batter. (*Do not* overfill. Each cone should have no more than 1/4 cup of batter.) Bake for 20 minutes at 350°F. Cool completely. Frost and decorate with sprinkles. These treats are best served on the day they are made.

Mom's Flag Cake

This is my all-time favorite cake from my mom's kitchen.

1 package chocolate cake mix
12-ounce can sweetened condensed milk
Whipped topping, thawed

Blueberries
Strawberries or raspberries

Prepare cake mix according to package directions. Bake as directed in 13 x 9 x 2-inch pan. While the cake is still warm, poke holes in top with the end of a wooden spoon and pour the evaporated milk over it evenly. Cool completely in the refrigerator. (It's best if it chills overnight.) Frost the top of the cake with whipped topping. Decorate it with fruit to look like a flag with blueberries in the star area and strawberries or raspberries to form stripes. Refrigerate until serving time. Yum!

Father's Day
Third Sunday in June

Key Verse

I have no greater joy than to hear that my children are walking in the truth. (3 John 4)

A Little History

Honor your father and your mother, as the LORD your God has commanded you, so that you may live long and that it may go well with you. (Deuteronomy 5:16)

On the third Sunday in June, fathers across the United States are honored by their children in commemoration of Father's Day. They are given cards and presents, treated to a special dinner and, often, a restful day in their favorite spots: the recliner.

There is some controversy about who actually came up with the idea of Father's Day, but there's little disagreement that the strongest promoter of the holiday was Sonora Smart Dodd of Spokane, Washington. Sonora's mother had died at a young age, leaving her father to raise six children alone. She felt that her dad, Civil War veteran Henry Jackson Smart, was an outstanding father, and she wanted to do something to honor him.[18]

After listening to a Mother's Day sermon in 1909, Mrs. Dodd asked that her minister dedicate a church service to honor her father on his birthday, June 5. The minister was unable to prepare the service so quickly and the service was postponed to June 19. This was the birth of the first Father's Day.[19]

In subsequent years, children in Washington began to honor their fathers on the third Sunday in June with gifts and visits. It wasn't long before the movement spread to other states, and in 1924 President Calvin Coolidge made Father's Day a national event.[20] Then, in 1966 President Lyndon Johnson signed a presidential proclamation declaring the third Sunday of June as Father's Day.[21]

Today, Father's Day offers children of all ages an opportunity to honor their dads. Father's Day even has a special flower: the rose. Red roses are traditionally worn by children whose fathers are living, and a white rose signifies that one's father has died.[22] Father's Day has become an important American tradition in recognition of the sacrifices men make for their families.

A Closer Look

By wisdom a house is built,
and through understanding it is established. (Proverbs 24:3)

When President Calvin Coolidge made Father's Day a national event in 1924, the purpose was to "establish more intimate relations between fathers and their children and to impress upon fathers the full measure of their obligations."[23] The President's words are very much in line with what God requires of both fathers and their children.

A Child's Responsibility

A wise son brings joy to his father. (Proverbs 10:1)

One of the best ways a child can honor his or her parents is by pursuing wisdom. And as Christians, we know that true wisdom comes from God. Through prayer and the study of God's Word, we develop an intimate relationship with Him and have access to the wisdom necessary to guide our lives as well as our relationships.

As we seek the heart of God, we will be given the knowledge and discernment to honor our parents, even in a relationship where a parent may not be a believer. Even when a parent and child share a common faith, the pressures and temptations of the world can strain relationships. Part of honoring parents is putting bitterness or perceived wrongs aside and forgiving even those who may not realize or acknowledge an offense.

Bear with each other and forgive whatever grievances you may have against one another. Forgive as the Lord forgave you. (Colossians 3:13)

A Father's Responsibility

Fathers, do not exasperate your children; instead, bring them up in the training and instruction of the Lord. (Ephesians 6:4)

Fathers have an obligation to train and instruct their children in the faith and to do it without "exasperating" them. As the parent of teenagers in the throes of hormonal mood swings, I know this seems like an impossible task. God is fully aware that we are not up to the challenge, but He is. In fact, the best parenting is done on our knees. Through our fervent prayers and daily dependence on God, our children will see in our lives a living faith that will guide them through their lives.

I always get a little teary when I look at photos of my husband, son and father-in-law at a gathering of Promise Keepers they attended together in Washington, DC. To see how faith has been passed down through the generations brings great joy to me and still touches my husband very deeply. The relationship between a father and son who are also brothers in Christ is a bond that will never be broken. And, as the Bible tells us, nothing brings a father more joy than to know that his children are walking with the Lord.

Table Talk

- What do you admire most about your father?
- What do you appreciate most about being a father?
- What is the best advice your father ever gave you? What's the best advice you've ever given your children?

- What are the dreams you have for each of your children?

Celebrate!

Preschool and Above

- Using fabric paint, decorate a T-shirt for Dad to let him know he is special. Decorate the shirt with handprints, drawings, a self portrait, whatever. Just be sure to date and sign it.
- Draw a picture of a favorite activity that you do with your dad or a favorite memory that you have of him. A copy shop can often make a drawing into a calendar, key chain, coffee mug or other item so that your dad will have a daily reminder of your time together.

Elementary Age and Above

- Instead of a traditional Father's Day card, give Dad a big hug that he can take with him! Measure and cut a long strip of paper the length of a child's arm span. Use colorful markers to write the things you just love about your dad.
- Assemble a bucket of fun for Dad. Get a large bucket (an old five-gallon bucket will work fine) and fill it with treats and things Dad likes to do. For example, if he likes to fish, fill the bucket with the fixin's for a picnic lunch. Then slip in his fishing pole and maybe some new tackle. Don't forget to hang a "gone fishin'" sign from the bucket!

Teens and Above

- Put together a scrapbook of memories you and your Dad share. Be sure to include your feelings and observations about the events.
- Give your dad a certificate for a day or evening out together. You could go to dinner and a movie or spend a day hiking or fishing together.

Recipes to Enjoy

Father's Day Pancakes

What dad wouldn't be delighted with this morning treat?

>   3 cups buttermilk baking mix
>   1 cup milk
>   1 t. vanilla
>   1/2 cup strawberry preserves
>   1/2 cup maple syrup

Mix baking mix, milk and vanilla. Pour about 1/4 cup batter onto the hot griddle. Cook until pancakes bubble and are dry around the edges. Flip. Cook until golden brown on the other side. While pancakes cook, microwave the preserves until they're liquid, about 30 seconds. Add maple syrup, warm in the microwave and serve with the pancakes.

"My Hero" Sandwich

What better way to let Dad know he is a true hero?

One loaf French bread
Assorted deli meats and cheeses (salami, ham, turkey, provolone, etc.)
Lettuce leaves
Sliced tomato
Sliced cucumbers
Sliced onions
Mayonnaise
Italian salad dressing

Cut the bread in half lengthwise and spread both halves with mayonnaise. Pile with deli meats and cheeses. Add veggies. Dress with Italian dressing. Cut into slices to serve. Serve with dill pickles and chips and enjoy with your real hero.

Marinated Steak and Roasted Vegetables

For a "steak and potatoes" man, you can't beat this easy dinner.

1/2 cup oil
1/4 cup red wine vinegar
1/4 cup soy sauce
2 T. lemon juice
1 T. Dijon mustard
1 T. Worcestershire sauce
1 heaping t. minced garlic
1/4 t. black pepper
2 lbs. sirloin steak
Assorted vegetables (corn-on-the-cob, potatoes, zucchini, onions, baby carrots, etc.)
2 T. butter or margarine
Heavy duty aluminum foil

Mix the first eight ingredients to make a marinade. Put the marinade in a zippered bag with the meat. Marinate the meat in the refrigerator for several hours or overnight. Grill meat to desired internal temperature.

Cut the vegetables into chunks. Season with salt, pepper and margarine. Wrap in a double layer of aluminum foil. Place on the grill over medium heat and cook until the vegetables are tender, about 25-30 minutes.

Triple Chocolate Brownies

1 package brownie mix
1/2 cup semi-sweet chocolate chips
1/2 cup white chocolate chips

Prepare brownie mix according to package directions. Stir semi-sweet chocolate and white chocolate chips into batter. Bake according to package directions. When cool, dust with powdered sugar and cut into squares. Enjoy!

Notes

1. "The History of Flag Day" [on-line], November 18, 2002. Available from: <http://www.usflag.org/flag.day.html>.
2. Ibid.
3. "Betsy Ross" [on-line], November 18, 2002. Available from: <http://www.usflag.org/about.betsy.ross.html>.
4. "About the US Flag Code" [on-line], November 18, 2002. Available from: <http://www.usflag.org/us.code36.html>.
5. "What Do the Colors of the Flag Mean?" [on-line], November 18, 2002. Available from: <http://www.usflag.org/colors.html>.
6. "The Original Pledge of Allegiance" [on-line], November 18, 2002. Available from: <http://www.usflag.org/pledgeofallegiance.html>.
7. Ibid.
8. Ibid.
9. Office of the Press Secretary, "President Signs Housing Assistance and Pledge of Allegiance Bills" [on-line], November 13, 2002. November 18, 2002. Available from: <http://www.whitehouse.gov/news/releases/2002/11/20021113-12.html>.
10. *Newsday*, "Bush Signs Bill on God References" [on-line], November 13, 2002. November 18, 2002. Available from: <http://www.newsday.com/news/politics/wire/sns-ap-bush-under-god1113nov13>. Archived article.
11. "Flag Flying Etiquette, Care, etc." [on-line], November 18, 2002. Available from: <http://www.capitolflags.com/etiquette.html>.
12. "The Star Spangled Banner" [on-line], November 18, 2002. Available from: <http://www.usembassy.de/usa/etexts/gov/anthem.pdf>.
13. Frances Scott Key, "The Star Spangled Banner" [on-line], November 18, 2002. Available from: <http://www.usembassy.de/usa/etexts/gov/anthem.htm>.
14. "What Do the Colors of the Flag Mean?"
15. "RestoreMyFreedom.com, Quotes on Education" [on-line], November 18, 2002. Available from: <http://www.restoremyfreedom.com/quotes-education.html>.
16. "Flag Flying Etiquette, Care, etc."
17. Ibid.
18. Carol Barkin and Elizabeth James, *The Holiday Handbook* (New York: Clarion Books, 1994), p. 160.
19. Ibid.
20. Elizabeth Berg, *Family Traditions* (Pleasantville, NY: The Reader's Digest Association, 1992), p. 80.
21. Ibid.
22. "History of Father's Day" [on-line], January 24, 2004. Available from: <http://gcards.com/fathersday/history.html>.
23. Berg, p. 80.

July

Hebrew: **Tammuz** (see Jeremiah 39:2)

Independence Day
July 4

Their sorrow was turned into joy and their mourning into a day of **celebration***. (Esther 9:22)*

Independence Day

July 4

Key Verse

Unless the LORD builds the house,
its builders labor in vain. (Psalm 127:1)

A Little History

We hold these truths to be self-evident, that all men are created equal, that they are endowed by their Creator with certain unalienable rights, that among these are life, liberty and the pursuit of happiness. . . . And for the support of this declaration, with a firm reliance on the protection of divine Providence, we mutually pledge to each other our lives, our fortunes and our sacred honor.

—The Declaration of Independence, 1776[1]

Independence Day is observed on July 4 in the United States with much fanfare and celebration to commemorate the signing of the Declaration of Independence from British rule in 1776. Citizens attend parades, shoot fireworks, wave flags and gather with friends and family to celebrate the birth of the United States of America.

Contrary to popular belief, there was little celebration on the first Independence Day. As the delegates to the Second Continental Congress left their assembly in Philadelphia, they were well aware that their actions were an official declaration of war on what was, at that time, the most powerful country in the world.[2]

Why were our founding fathers willing to stake "their lives, their fortunes and their sacred honor"[3] to win freedom from Britain? The answer to this question is best understood through their own words, spoken as America declared her freedom and shaped the government of a country that still stands as a beacon to the world.

Samuel Adams, upon signing the Declaration of Independence, 1776:

We have this day restored the Sovereign, to whom men ought to be obedient. He reigns in heaven and . . . from the rising to the setting sun, may His kingdom come.[4]

John Adams, in a letter to his wife upon signing the Declaration of Independence, 1776:

[This day] . . . will be the most memorable . . . in the history of America. I am apt to believe that it will be celebrated by succeeding generations, as the great anniversary festival. It ought to be commemorated as the Day of Deliverance, by solemn acts of devotion to God Almighty. It ought to be solemnized with pomp and parade, with shows, games, sports, guns, bells, bonfires and illuminations, from one end of this continent to the other, from this time forward forevermore.

You may think me transported with enthusiasm, but I am not. I am well aware of the toil and blood and treasure that it will cost to maintain this Declaration, and support and defend these States. Yet through all the gloom, I can see the rays of ravishing light and glory. I can see that the end is worth all the means.[5]

Benjamin Franklin, addressing the Constitutional Convention, 1787:

In the beginning of the contest with Great Britain, when we were sensible of danger, we had daily prayer in this room for Divine protection. Our prayers were heard, and they were graciously answered. . . . Have we forgotten this powerful Friend? Or do we imagine we no longer need His assistance? I have lived a long time, and the longer I live, the more convincing proofs I see of this truth—that God governs in the affairs of men. If a sparrow cannot fall to the ground without His notice, is it probable that an empire can rise without His aid?

I firmly believe that without His concurring aid, we shall succeed in this political building no better than the builders of Babel. . . . I therefore beg leave to move—that henceforth prayers imploring the assistance of heaven, and its blessings on our deliberations, be held in this Assembly every morning before we proceed to business.[6]

Franklin's motion was immediately adopted and, after a three-day recess for fasting and prayer, the Assembly convened and drafted the Constitution that still governs our nation. To this day, all sessions of Congress are opened with prayer.

James Madison, fourth President and chief author of the US Constitution, 1787:

Without the intervention of God there never would have been a Constitution.[7]

George Washington, addressing the nation upon leaving office as President, 1796:

Reason and experience both forbid us to expect that national morality can prevail in exclusion of religious principle.[8]

John Adams, second President of the United States:

Our Constitution was made only for a moral and religious people. It is wholly inadequate to the government of any other. We have no government armed with power capable of contending with human passions unbridled by morality and religion.[9]

Thomas Jefferson, inscribed on the Jefferson Memorial, Washington, DC:

God who gave us life, gave us liberty. Can the liberties of a nation be secure when we have removed a conviction that these liberties are a gift of God? Indeed I tremble for my country when I reflect that God is just, that His justice cannot sleep forever.[10]

A Closer Look

A nation which does not remember what it was yesterday, does not know what it is today, nor what it is trying to do. We are trying to do a futile thing if we do not know where we came from or what we have been about.

—Woodrow Wilson, 1913[11]

Those who helped shape our nation were people of deep, personal faith. They knew the truth that has been purged from many of our history books: that America was forged by dependence upon God and that her future is in His hands.

We enjoy great freedom as citizens of the United States. We have been so blessed by God that our young nation stands as the world's "superpower." We enjoy wealth and opportunity unmatched anywhere else on earth. But with this freedom comes a responsibility to pass on our nation's godly heritage to our children.

A.W. Tozer said, "In the sight of God we are judged not so much by what we do as by our reasons for doing it."[12] Our founding fathers' deep personal faith in God translated into a vision for America. It's our responsibility that our children, and their children's children, understand this vision along with the events leading to the birth of America.

On April 5, 1993, the cover of *Time* magazine read "The Generation That Forgot God."[13] Will you allow this to ring true for future generations? As you prepare for the Fourth of July this year, make a commitment to put God, and our nation's godly heritage, at the forefront of your celebration. America's future depends on it!

> *If the foundations are destroyed,*
> *What can the righteous do? (Psalm 11:3, NASB)*

Table Talk

- What does freedom mean to you?
- What freedoms do we have in the United States that aren't available to people in other parts of the world?
- Why do you think the people who signed the Declaration of Independence were willing to stake everything they had to break free from British rule?
- Do you agree with Benjamin Franklin that "God governs in the affairs of men" specifically in the area of government? Why or why not?

Celebrate!

Preschool and Above

- Attend an Independence Day parade or have one of your own. Ask your neighbors to decorate bikes, wagons, strollers and of course themselves. If you like, ask participants to wear red, white or blue T-shirts and march as a traveling flag!
- Avoid the danger of fireworks with young children by taping bubble wrap to the ground and having the kids jump on it.

Elementary Age and Above

- Read about our nation's godly heritage. You might try reading *The Light and the Glory for Children: Discovering God's Plan for America from Christopher Columbus to George Washing-*

ton and *From Sea to Shining Sea* by Peter Marshall and David Manuel, *In God We Trust: Stories of Faith in American History* by Timothy Crater and Ranelda Hunsicker, as well as *America: Built on Character, Founded on Faith* by Mark Ammerman Another great book on You may also want to check your Christian bookstore for more choices.

Teens and Above

• Commit to praying for our government leaders. You can receive prayer requests directly from the President by signing up for the Presidential Prayer Team at www. presidentialprayerteam.org or calling 520.797.7173.

Recipes to Enjoy!

Berry Overload Pancakes

Gently fold blueberries and raspberries into your favorite pancake recipe or mix and cook as directed. True berry lovers even serve these with berry syrup!

Red, White and Bleu Salad

1 8-ounce package penne pasta, cooked, drained and cooled
1 cup chunky bleu cheese dressing
2 cups grape tomatoes (or cherry tomatoes), halved
1/2 cup red onion, chopped

Mix all ingredients together. Chill and serve.

Old Glory Cake

2 baked 8- or 9-inch round white cake layers
2 cups boiling water, divided
1 3-ounce package gelatin, any red flavor
1 3-ounce package gelatin, any blue flavor
1 8-ounce container whipped topping, thawed

After baking the cake layers and cooling them for ten minutes, remove the cake from the pans. Wash the cake pans and then return the cake layers to the pans. Pierce the cake layers with a large fork at 1/2-inch intervals. Stir 1 cup of the boiling water into red and blue gelatin in separate bowls until completely dissolved. Carefully pour the red gelatin over one cake layer and the blue gelatin over the second cake layer. Refrigerate for 3 hours.

Remove cakes from refrigerator. Dip the first cake pan in warm water for about 10 seconds, then transfer the cake onto a serving plate. Spread generously with whipped topping. Dip the second cake pan in warm water for about 10 seconds and carefully place the second cake layer on top of the first. Frost the top and sides of the cake with whipped topping. Refrigerate the cake for at least one hour before serving. Decorate with blueberries and raspberries or strawberries, if desired.

Independence Day Lemonade

3 cans lemonade concentrate
Red and blue food coloring
3 pitchers (clear are best)

Prepare lemonade as directed in three pitchers. Tint two of the pitchers red and blue. Cool and serve.

Texas BBQ

My friend Floy gave me the recipe for this yummy make-ahead dish. I added the red pepper for a little zip!

4-5 lb. beef brisket
4 T. Liquid Smoke
1 T. meat tenderizer
1/2 t. nutmeg
1/3 cup brown sugar
1 t. paprika
1 t. onion salt
1 t. garlic salt
1 t. celery salt
1/2 t. salt
1/4 t. pepper
1/4 t. red pepper (optional)
1/4 cup catsup

Marinate the brisket in liquid smoke and meat tenderizer for three hours or overnight. (Be sure to keep the fat side up so the marinade soaks into the meat.)

Remove the brisket from the marinade. Mix the rest of the ingredients and spread over the brisket. Wrap meat tightly in a double layer of foil with the seam up. Bake at 300°F for two hours. Cool before slicing. Pour juices over top when serving.

NOTE: You can also make this dish ahead and freeze the sliced meat in the juices. On the day you plan to serve it, thaw the meat completely, then warm it in the oven for 30 minutes.

Notes

1. "The Declaration of Independence: A Transcription" [on-line], January 24, 2004. Available from: <http://www.archives.gov/national_archives_experience/declaration_transcript.html>.
2. Charles Crismier, *Renewing the Soul of America* (Richmond, VA: Elijah Books, 2002), p. 309.
3. "The Declaration of Independence: A Transcription."
4. Peter Marshall and David Manuel, *The Light and the Glory* (Grand Rapids, MI: Fleming H. Revell, 1977), p. 309.
5. Ibid., pp. 310-11.
6. Crismier, p. 26-7.
7. Ibid., p. 27.
8. Ibid., p. 62.

9. Ibid., p. 64.
10. Ibid..
11. Ibid., p. 28.
12. A.W. Tozer, *The Root of the Righteous* (Camp Hill, PA: Christian Publications, Inc., 1986), p. 89.
13. Crismier, p. 33.

August

Hebrew: **Ab** (see Numbers 33:38)

*August is a month with no "official" holidays,
but that's no reason to cease celebrating! It provides an
excellent opportunity to explore one of my favorite celebrations:*

Birthdays!

And don't forget, there's always Sister's Day on August 5, Middle Child's Day on August 12 and Left Hander's Day on August 13.

May she who gave you birth **rejoice***!*
(Proverbs 23:25)

Birthdays

Key Verse

For you created my inmost being;
you knit me together in my mother's womb. . . .
All the days ordained for me
were written in your book
before one of them came to be. (Psalm 139:13, 16)

A Little History

She gave birth to her firstborn, a son. She wrapped him in cloths and placed him in a manger. (Luke 2:7)

What a party! Angels, shepherds, wise men all gathered to celebrate the birth of God's own Son! The birth of Jesus was the ultimate birthday party, and Christians around the world still look forward to this celebration all year long!

Early records indicate that birthday celebrations have been a part of our culture for thousands of years. The Bible notes a feast in honor of Pharaoh's birthday (see Genesis 40:20), family birthday celebrations by Job's sons (see Job 1:4, Amp.) as well as a party in honor of King Herod's birthday (see Matthew 14:6).

In pagan cultures, people thought the anniversary of one's birth allowed evil spirits to visit them, so family and friends would gather around the person with gifts and good wishes as protection.[1] As missionaries moved to these lands to spread the message of the gospel, new Christians were encouraged to move their celebrations from the anniversary of their own births to the feast day of the saint for which they were named.[2] The Church hoped this would help the new believers focus on the blessings of God and do away with their superstitious practices.

Today, birthday celebrations are enjoyed by both children and adults. Parties generally include a gathering of family and friends, gifts, games and, of course, a flaming birthday cake.

Here are how some of our birthday traditions originated:

- Children's birthday parties began as a German tradition called "Kinderfeste." *Kinder* means "children" and *feste* means "party."[3]

- Many historians also credit the birthday cake to the Germans. Sweet bread in the shape of the swaddling clothes the baby Jesus wore would be presented to the birthday person with a large candle in the middle to symbolize "the light of life."[4] The candle, which would be burned a little each year, had lines and numbers to signify the person's age until he was twelve years old. When the candle was blown out, the smoke was supposed to bring the birthday person's wishes to heaven as in Psalm 141:2: "May my prayer be set before you like incense."

- The famous "Happy Birthday" song was written in 1859 by two sisters. Mildred Hill composed the music and her sister Patti wrote the words.[5]
- The custom of sending birthday cards began in England about 100 years ago. Originally cards were sent as an apology for not being able to visit someone in person on his special day. Currently, birthday cards rank at the top of greeting card sales.[6]

A Closer Look

Jesus declared, "I tell you the truth, no one can see the kingdom of God unless he is born again." (John 3:3)

Birthdays are fun, but the real occasion we have to celebrate is the day we were "born again," when we were accepted into God's family through a profession of faith. Celebrating the anniversary of a person's "rebirth" into the family of God can become a very meaningful tradition as well as a fun way to reinforce one of the pillars of the Christian faith.

One of the best ways to teach this truth is using Jesus' words to Nicodemus, found in John 3:1-21. This passage concludes with the powerful message of salvation through faith alone. It provides a natural opportunity to ask the question, "If you stood before God today, would He allow you to enter heaven?" And, "If so, why?"

Families can then take the opportunity to reinforce the good news that we are saved through God's grace alone. God loves us so much that He sent Jesus to earth to live the perfect life that we can't. Jesus then paid the penalty for our sins by dying on the cross. All we need to do is go before Him in prayer, admit our sins and accept our need for His forgiveness through Jesus. This is how we are born again. What a reason to celebrate!

Table Talk

- What is your favorite birthday memory? Why is this special to you?
- Ask other family members to share a quality they especially appreciate and/or admire about the birthday person.
- Read Psalm 139:13-16. How do you feel when you hear God speaking these words about you before you were even born?
- We have all been born once through our mothers, but Jesus says in the Bible that we must be born again. What does this mean? Have you been born again?

Celebrate!

Preschool and Above

- In Holland, family members decorate the birthday person's chair at the dining room table. Use crepe paper, flowers (real or silk), ribbons, whatever you have on hand to make a "seat of honor" on the person's special day.
- Try the Israeli custom where small children sit on a chair while grown-ups raise and lower the chair one time for each year of the child's age. (This sounds like much more fun than the custom of the birthday spanking!)
- Enjoy the Chinese custom of eating noodles for lunch. Long noodles are served to wish the person a long life.

Elementary Age and Above

- Use fabric paint on a piece of canvas to create a special flag for the birthday person. In Denmark, families fly a flag outside to let everyone know that someone inside is celebrating a birthday.
- Take part in a 300-year-old birthday party tradition from Mexico by making a piñata! A piñata is a large papier-mâché object, usually in the shape of an animal or flower, filled with candy and small toys. The piñata is hung by a rope and then blindfolded children take turns trying to break it open with a stick. When they do, the treats spill out and the children scramble to gather them up. What fun!

    Here are the instructions for making your own piñata:

    You'll need:

    - Large, round balloon
    - Newspaper
    - White "school" glue
    - Water
    - Tempura paint
    - Crepe paper
    - String or fishing line
    - Small toys and/or candy

    Instructions:

1. This is a really messy project, so cover your work surface. An old shower curtain or piece of plastic works well. You can also lay down several layers of newspaper to cover the surface.
2. Tear several newspaper pages into strips about one inch wide and 6-8 inches long. Set these aside.
3. Next, in a medium-sized bowl prepare papier-mâché paste using one part glue to two parts water.

4. Blow up the balloon and tie it closed. You may want to set it in a bowl or cup to keep it steady while you work.
5. Dip the newspaper strips into the papier-mâché paste and spread them onto the balloon. Completely cover the balloon, leaving a hole at the top. Make the hole just big enough to allow you to put the treats in the piñata. Let the first layer of papier-mâché dry.
6. Add two more layers of newspaper strips and glue to your balloon. Allow each layer to dry completely in between. Once all layers are dry, pop the balloon.
7. Decorate your piñata with brightly colored paint. You can decorate it with designs or make it look like an animal such as a fish. When the paint dries, you can also hang streamers from your piñata.
8. Poke some small holes near the top and thread a piece of string or fishing line through each hole and tie the two ends together to make a "handle." Thread a longer piece of rope through the "handle" to tie the piñata up.
9. Fill the piñata with treats, tie it up and let the kids swing away!

Teens and Above

• Instead of a birthday cake, take part in the Russian custom of preparing a special birthday pie. Use your favorite recipe for a two-crust pie, with one exception: Carve birthday wishes into the top crust before baking.

• Try a Filipino tradition and string blinking colored lights inside and outside the house to announce to the neighborhood that a birthday is being celebrated. In the Philippines, the lights are turned on in the early evening after the family has gone to church together to thank God for the birthday person.

• Make up a birthday greeting and set it to a favorite tune. Or you could make a music video. If you don't have musical accompaniment, the music for many popular songs is available on karaoke tapes.

Recipes to Enjoy

Jelly and Ice Cream

This is a traditional birthday treat in England. But the name is a bit misleading: The "jelly" is actually gelatin.

    1 6-ounce package of fruit-flavored gelatin mix
    1 quart vanilla ice cream
    Nonpareils (colored candy balls used for cake decorating)

Prepare gelatin according to the instructions on the packet. Chill until firm. Spoon the gelatin into individual serving dishes and top with ice cream. Sprinkle with nonpareils.

Bolitas de Nuez

These little treats, translated as "small balls of nuts," are a sweet tradition at birthday celebrations in Mexico.

2 cups ground pecans
1 cup powdered sugar
2 egg whites, stiffly beaten

Mix pecans with sugar. Gently add beaten egg whites. Shape mixture into balls. Bake on a buttered baking sheet at 350°F for 5 minutes.

Dump Cake

Cooks of any level can make this delicious birthday cake! Just dump, bake and enjoy!

White or yellow cake mix
1 large can cherry pie filling
1 large can crushed pineapple, undrained
1 cup chopped nuts
1 stick of butter or margarine, melted

Grease a 9 x 13-inch pan. Pour the pineapple into the pan. Cover with the cherry pie filling and then sprinkle the top with the cake mix and nuts. Pour the melted butter or margarine over everything. Bake at 350°F for 45 minutes or until golden brown.

Birthday Balloons

This fun treat will appeal to those pesky "cake haters" of the world as well as those of us who enjoy sweets in any form!

Cookie dough (homemade or refrigerated), any flavor
White frosting (homemade or canned)
Food coloring
Assorted small candies (M&Ms, gumdrops, etc.)
Small tube of decorating gel
String licorice
Stiff cardboard, large flat tray or cookie sheet
Foil

Roll out cookie dough and cut into several balloon shapes. Bake and cool. Cover cardboard or cookie sheet with foil. Divide frosting into several bowls and tint to make deep colors. Frost cookies and decorate with candies. Use decorating gel to write messages, if desired. Arrange balloons on the prepared tray in a "bunch" and use licorice as strings. Use a small piece of licorice to tie the balloon bunch together. Up, up and away!

Notes

1. "Birthday Traditions Around the World" [on-line], November 12, 2002. Available from: <http://www.cyberkisses.com/Birthday/birth-traditions.html>.

2. "Traditions from Around the World" [on-line], November 12, 2002. Available from: <http://www.birthdaycelebrations.net/traditions.htm>.

3. "Birthday Traditions Around the World."

4. Ibid.

5. "Fun Facts About 'Happy Birthday to You'" [on-line], February 21, 2003. Available from: <http://www.ibiblio.org/team/fun/birthday/>.

6. "History of Birthdays" [on-line], November 12, 2002. Available from: <www.celebrateexpress.com/bexpress/planning/BirthdayCelebrations.asp>.

September

Hebrew: **Elul** (see Nehemiah 6:15)

Labor Day
1st Monday in September

They **celebrated** *the feast for seven days.*
(Nehemiah 8:18)

Labor Day
1st Monday in September

Key Verse

All hard work brings a profit,
but mere talk leads only to poverty. (Proverbs 14:23)

A Little History

Not gold, but only man can make
  A people great and strong;
Men who for truth and honor's sake,
  Stand fast and suffer long.

Brave men who work while others sleep,
  Who dare while others fly—
They build a nation's pillars deep
  And lift them to the sky."
        —"Great Men" by Ralph Waldo Emerson[1]

Labor Day was begun by labor unions in the late nineteenth century as a way of recognizing and honoring the achievements of American workers. There is some disagreement about the identity of the true founder of the holiday. Some say it is Peter J. McGuire, the leader of the Brotherhood of Carpenters and Joiners, while others claim it is Matthew Maguire, a machinist and labor leader in New Jersey.[2] We do know, however, where the first Labor Day celebration was held: New York City. The event was organized by the Central Labor Union as

> a street parade to exhibit to the public the strength and esprit de corps of the trade and labor organizations followed by a festival for the recreation and amusement of the workers and their families.[3]

On September 5, 1882, the first Labor Day celebration was kicked off with a parade through the streets of New York City. Twenty thousand workers marched up Broadway carrying banners that read "Labor Creates All Wealth!" and "Eight hours for work! Eight hours for rest! And eight hours for recreation!" After the parade, there were picnics all around the city where families feasted on Irish stew, homemade bread and apple pie. In the evening, they watched a fireworks display.[4]

Sounds fun, doesn't it? Well, it wasn't long before the idea of Labor Day spread from coast to coast. In 1894, Congress made Labor Day official by designating the first Monday in September as a federal holiday.[5]

Today, Americans enjoy Labor Day weekend as a welcome respite and "last blast of summer" before autumn arrives. They often celebrate the holiday with picnics and family gatherings. Elaborate Labor Day parades are not as common as they were in the past, but labor leaders still use the occasion as a way to publicize the contribution of workers to the nation's economy and well-being.

A Closer Look

Work is not what we do for a living, but what we do with our living.
—William J. Bennett, Former US Secretary of Education[6]

It's a little known fact that in 1909 the American Federation of Labor designated the Sunday before Labor Day as "Labor Sunday" with the intention of furthering the "spiritual and educational aspects of the labor movement."[7] This act indicates that the founders of Labor Day realized that worker loyalty and satisfaction involved much more than collecting a paycheck. They recognized that work quickly becomes drudgery if the worker cannot see the higher purpose behind it.

The Labor Day holiday provides families with a natural opportunity to pass on important truths about work on what is generally a day of leisure. Although they may never admit it, our children need to understand the value of work (whether paid or unpaid), as well as experience the joy that comes from a job well done. The best place to begin this lesson is in God's Word.

The Bible has *a lot* to teach us about work, and it starts right from the beginning. Genesis 2 tells us that the first thing God did after creating man was to give him the job of tending the garden and caring for the animals (see 2:15). God noticed that as Adam was naming the animals that he needed help (see 2:19-20), so He created Eve, divinely ordaining the first employee work group (see 2:21-22). So even in the perfect world of the Garden of Eden, where everything was provided, God knew that we need to work.

A quick scan of a New International Version concordance shows that the Bible uses the word *work* 394 times and has an additional 93 references to *labor*. From "balance" to "laziness" to the identity of our true "boss," God's Word provides a comprehensive employee manual. Take a look:

- "For six days, work is to be done, but the seventh day is a Sabbath of rest, holy to the LORD." (Exodus 31:15)
- "The sluggard's craving will be the death of him,/ because his hands refuse to work." (Proverbs 21:25)
- "Do you see a man skilled at his work?/ He will serve before kings;/ he will not serve before obscure men." (22:29)
- "She sets about her work vigorously;/ her arms are strong for her tasks." (31:17)
- "Always give yourselves fully to the work of the Lord, because you know that your labor in the Lord is not in vain." (1 Corinthians 15:58)

- "Whatever you do, work at it with all your heart, as working for the Lord, not for men." (Colossians 3:23)
- "Make it your ambition to lead a quiet life, to mind your own business and to work with your hands, just as we told you, so that your daily life may win the respect of outsiders and so that you will not be dependent on anybody." (1 Thessalonians 4:11-12)
- "If a man will not work, he shall not eat." (2 Thessalonians 3:10)

Table Talk

- What is your "dream" job? Why?
- How can a person discover the "life work" God has for him or her?
- Is it possible to make work an idol in our lives? What are some examples?
- Why do you think God established the Sabbath?
- What does it mean practically to work "for the Lord, not for men" (Colossians 3:23)? Can you think of any examples?
- How can we glorify God through our work?

Celebrate!

Preschool and Above

- Attend a Labor Day parade in your community or plan one in your neighborhood. Ask children and/or adults to come dressed as people from different careers: firefighter, baseball player, nurse, construction worker, etc. Decorate bikes with streamers and wave flags to celebrate how different occupations contribute to the community. You might even be able to convince your local fire station to lead the parade with a fire engine, sirens and all!

Elementary Age and Above

- Prepare and deliver a treat to someone who has to work on Labor Day, like a firefighter, a police officer or a hospital worker.
- Collect photos and other items to put together a scrapbook about your summer activities. Be sure to include your thoughts about how God blessed you during the summer.

Teens and Above

- Take a personality and spiritual gifts assessment together as a family and explore different careers that make the most of the way God created you.
- Contact someone you know who is working in a career that interests you and ask if you can "shadow" him or her for a day (or half day) to see what the job is really like.

Recipes to Enjoy

Lazy Day BBQ

3 lbs. (or enough to feed your family) chicken pieces
Assorted vegetables (corn-on-the-cob, potatoes, onions and green pepper cut
   into chunks, carrots, etc.)
Seasoning salt
BBQ sauce
Heavy-duty foil

Season the chicken and vegetables with seasoning salt. Wrap the chicken in a double layer of foil and seal tightly with the seam on top. Do the same with the vegetables. Cook the packets on the grill over medium heat until the chicken is cooked through (juices run clear) and the vegetables are tender (50-60 minutes is usually enough for the chicken, less for the vegetables). Pour warm BBQ sauce over the chicken and toss the vegetables with butter or margarine.

"Last Blast of Summer" Cake

1 yellow cake mix
1 can white frosting (fluffy, whipped frosting is best)
Food coloring
Black decorating icing
Candy corn
Child's sunglasses (side "ear pieces" removed)

Prepare the cake mix according to the package directions. Bake in two 8- or 9-inch round pans according to the package directions. Cool and remove cakes from pans.

Tint the frosting with yellow food coloring. Frost the cake. Decorate the top of the cake as a smiling sun, using candy corn on the outer edge for "rays" and black decorator icing for the smile. Put the sunglasses on the cake as a finishing touch.

Notes

1. William J. Bennett, ed., *The Book of Virtues* (New York: Simon and Schuster, 1993), p. 418.
2. "The History of Labor Day" [on-line], November 12, 2002. Available from: <http://www.dol.gov/opa/aboutdol/labor-day.htm>.
3. Ibid.
4. Cynthia Blair, "1882: First Labor Day Celebration Held at Union Square Park" [on-line], November 12, 2002. Available from: <http://www.newsday.com/other/special/ny-ihny0901story.htmlstory>.
5. "The Origins of Labor Day" [on-line], September 2, 2001. November 12, 2002. Available from: <http://www.pbs.org/newshour/bb/business/september96/labor_day_9-2.html>.
6. Bennett, p. 348.
7. "The History of Labor Day."

October

Hebrew: **Ethanim** (see 1 Kings 8:2)

Columbus Day
Second Monday in October

Halloween/Halloween Alternatives
October 31

[Celebrate] it for the generations to come.

(Exodus 31:16)

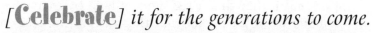

Columbus Day

Key Verse

The light shines in the darkness, but the darkness has not understood it. (John 1:5)

A Little History

For the LORD your God is bringing you into a good land—a land with streams and pools of water, with springs flowing in the valleys and hills. (Deuteronomy 8:7)

Columbus Day celebrates the discovery of America on October 12, 1492. Christopher Columbus, whose first name literally means "Christ bearer,"[1] felt very strongly that God had chosen him to bring the light of Christ to a dark world. He wrote in his journal: "It is though our Lord has set a fire in my soul. I feel His hand on me."[2]

Columbus was a navigator from Genoa, Italy. He had little formal schooling, but taught himself Portuguese, Spanish and Latin. Columbus was trained as a weaver in his father's business but was interested in the sea and as a young man spent much time at the busy Port of Genoa.[3]

Columbus believed that if he sailed 3,000 miles west he would reach Asia, thus discovering a shortcut to the West Indies. This was a radical concept, because navigators at that time felt that the world was flat, and following Columbus' plan would send a ship sailing off the edge of the earth. In fact, the idea seemed so preposterous that funding for the voyage was turned down by the rulers of England, France and Portugal. King Ferdinand and Queen Isabella of Spain also refused Columbus' request initially, only reconsidering the proposal at the persistent urging of their priest.[4]

Columbus set sail with ninety sailors and three ships, the *Pinta*, the *Niña* and the *Santa Maria*, on August 3, 1492.[5] As the long voyage progressed, the crew of all three ships became frightened and frustrated because they hadn't yet reached land. They threatened to mutiny. Columbus convinced the men to hang on for three more days and promised that if they didn't see signs of land by then, they could turn back.[6]

Columbus wrote in his journal that only a miracle could save the expedition. He prayed, "I commit myself to You, Lord. Please complete what You have done and deliver me safely." The Lord answered his prayer, and in the early morning hours of the third day, the crew spotted land.[7]

Columbus first landed at what are now the Caribbean Islands, either Watling Island, Grand Turk Island or Samana Cay.[8] As recorded in his journal, he named the island San Salvador, which means "Holy Savior," and bowed on the beach with his crew, praying:

O Lord, Almighty and Everlasting God, by Your word You created the heaven and the earth and the sea. Thank You for choosing to use us, Your humble servants, in making Your name known in this second part of the earth.[9]

There are no records of any celebrations to commemorate Columbus' discovery in the 300 years following his successful landing in the New World. Then in 1792 a monument was dedicated to him in New York City.[10] Soon after that, the city of Washington was officially named the District of Columbia and became the capital of the United States.[11] The Columbian Exposition in Chicago in 1892 featured replicas of Columbus's three ships.[12]

On October 12, 1866, the Italian population of New York City organized the first celebration of the discovery of America out of pride for their native son. The idea soon spread across the country and Italians in San Francisco came up with the name Columbus Day.[13]

Colorado became the first state to observe a Columbus Day in 1905. As other states followed, President Franklin Roosevelt officially proclaimed October 12 Columbus Day. In 1971, President Richard Nixon declared it a federal public holiday to be celebrated on the second Monday in October.[14]

In recent years, Columbus Day celebrations have become somewhat controversial. Some people feel Columbus' discovery of America and the subsequent conquest by Spain amounted to genocide for the natives. A movement is growing in many schools and communities to replace the celebration of Columbus Day with "Indigenous Peoples Day."[15]

Personally, I think this is a very sad turn of events for our nation. Although respect for other cultures is an important tenet of our society, and I do not condone the hardships that were forced on American natives, I believe celebrating the cultures of some of the native people Columbus encountered, which included pagan practices and atrocities, is very wrong.

My husband and I recently visited Mayan ruins on Mexico's Yucatan Peninsula. We learned that the Mayans practiced human sacrifice on a daily basis among their own people and with neighboring tribes. In fact, records show that the Mayans would even rip the heart from a person while he was still living in an effort to satisfy their "gods." Everywhere I turned there were carved images of who they considered to be their most powerful god: a serpent.

Was there a place more in need of the light of Christ? Praise God for the obedience of Christopher Columbus, the "Christ bearer" to the new world!

A Closer Look

It was the Lord who put into my mind (I could feel His hand upon me) the fact that it would be possible to sail from here to the Indies. All who heard of my project rejected it with laughter, ridiculing me. There is no question that the inspiration was from the Holy Spirit, because He comforted me with rays of inspiration from the Holy Scriptures.

—Journal of Christopher Columbus[16]

Columbus felt the call of God to undertake a project that the world considered ridiculous, and he made it his life's work to complete it. How many of us are willing to do the same?

I wonder if Columbus, like believers through the ages, wrestled with God's calling. Just listen to Moses' arguments in the book of Exodus as he stood at the burning bush:

- "Who am I, that I should go to Pharaoh and bring the Israelites out of Egypt?" (3:11)
- "Suppose I go to the Israelites and say to them, 'The God of your fathers has sent me to you,' and they ask me, 'What is his name?' Then what shall I tell them?" (3:13)
- "What if they do not believe me or listen to me and say, 'The LORD did not appear to you'?" (4:1)
- "O Lord, I have never been eloquent, neither in the past nor since you have spoken to your servant. I am slow of speech and tongue." (4:10)
- "O Lord, please send someone else to do it." (4:13)

To each of Moses concerns, Almighty God patiently gave him an answer. It wasn't until Moses asked God to send someone else that the Bible tells us: "Then the LORD's anger burned against Moses" (4:14).

God gives us numerous examples in the Bible where His people tried to wiggle out of their calling or, as in the case of the apostle Peter, responded immediately but lost their nerve when the going got rough. Peter's story is recorded in Matthew 14:22-31. Read through this account and you can see how Peter got himself into trouble by not having enough faith in Jesus. He did respond to Jesus' call, though, which is a step in the right direction. It was just that look into the wind that did him in and made his faith falter.

How have you responded to the call of God? Or, more important, how will you respond to His call in the future? Are you willing to put your life and reputation on the line for Jesus? If your answer is yes, just listen to Jesus' response to your courage:

> Blessed are you when men hate you,
>   when they exclude you and insult you
>   and reject your name as evil,
>   because of the Son of Man.
> Rejoice in that day and leap for joy, because great is your reward in heaven.
> (Luke 6:22-23)

Table Talk

- What are your dreams? What are you willing to risk to achieve them?
- Have you ever gone out on a limb for God? Tell about it.
- One of the things that attracted explorers to new lands was the promise of treasure. As Christians, where is our true treasure? And what are you doing to find and safeguard it?
- How can we discover God's will for our lives?

Celebrate!

Preschool and Above

- Take a walk around your neighborhood or a nearby park. When you get home, discuss what new discoveries you made.
- Make your own edible version of Columbus' ship! You will need:
    - 1/2 banana, cut lengthwise
    - 1 fruit roll-up snack
    - Toothpicks
    - Peanut butter (optional)

Spread the banana with peanut butter (if desired). Cut three triangles in a sheet of fruit roll-up to look like sails. Attach the sails to toothpicks and stick them in the banana. Yummy and fun!

Elementary Age and Above

- We know so much about Columbus' discovery of the new world because he kept detailed journals. Cover and decorate a blank notebook as your family's journal. Leave it in a convenient spot and encourage family members to jot down their activities, thoughts, feelings, questions or concerns each day. Plan a special time each week to share your journal entries with each other.

Teens and Above

- Research foods native to both the "old" and "new" worlds during Columbus' time. Prepare a meal or snack melding the two cultures.

Recipes to Enjoy

Discovery of the "new" world introduced many foods to Europe. These recipes will give your family an idea of what they would be missing if Columbus hadn't discovered America.

Baked Spaghetti Pie

Imagine: Italian pasta without tomato sauce! Lovers of Italian food owe the Incas and Aztec Indians for the introduction of tomatoes. And guess what? It took Europeans quite a while to try tomatoes because many people believed they were poisonous.

    1 8-ounce package of spaghetti, cooked and drained
    1 egg
    1/4 cup Parmesan cheese
    1/2 lb. hamburger or Italian sausage
    2 cups meatless spaghetti sauce
    1 cup mozzarella cheese

Mix the pasta, egg and Parmesan cheese together. Press the mixture into a greased pie plate. Brown the hamburger or sausage and add it to the spaghetti sauce. Put the sauce mixture on top of the pasta in the pie plate. Top with mozzarella cheese. Bake 25-30 minutes at 350°F until hot. Cut in wedges, like pie, to serve.

Tropical Fruit Salad

Put together a medley of tropical fruits native to the "new" world. Canned or frozen versions are also readily available at today's supermarkets.
Choose from:

- Kiwi
- Mangoes
- Pineapple
- Papaya
- Banana

Just cut up the fruit and mix together with a dash of orange, lemon or lime juice.

Potato Foccacia

Potatoes originated with the Incas of the Andes Mountains. The Spanish brought potatoes to Europe, where the English began to grow them on a large scale. English colonists brought the potato back to America after 1600.

1 loaf potato bread (found in most supermarket bakeries)
1/4 cup butter
Italian seasoning
Garlic salt

Cut bread in half horizontally. Spread with butter. Sprinkle with seasonings. Broil in oven until golden brown.

Lemonade

Lemons were a tart surprise for Europeans when they arrived in America.

1 large can lemonade concentrate
Lemon slices (enough for each glass)

Prepare lemonade according to package directions. Garnish each glass with a sliced lemon.

Chocolate Surprise Brownies

We can thank Native Americans for chocolate. In fact, the Mayans and Aztecs even used cocoa beans as a form of money.

Brownie mix
Chocolate peanut butter cups, small size, unwrapped
Mini-muffin tin

Prepare the brownie mix according to the package directions and then bake in the mini-muffin tin. As soon as the brownies come out of the oven, press the peanut butter cups into the middle of each brownie. Remove from pan. Sprinkle with powdered sugar when completely cool.

Halloween/Halloween Alternatives

October 31

Key Verse

For you were once darkness, but now you are light in the Lord. Live as children of light.
(Ephesians 5:8)

A Little History

For our struggle is not against flesh and blood, but against the rulers, against the authorities, against the powers of this dark world and against the spiritual forces of evil in the heavenly realms. (Ephesians 6:12)

Halloween is a very scary holiday, literally! The celebration has its roots in the pagan rites of an ancient Celtic religion called Druidism.[17] The Druids, then and now, worship the things of creation such as the earth, fire, sky, trees and animals. The majority of ancient Druids were concentrated on the British Isles—Ireland, Scotland and Wales.[18]

October 31 marks the last day of the year for Druids, and it is extremely sacred to them. On that date, Druidic worshipers pay tribute to Samhain, Lord of the Dead. Ancient Druids believed that the separation between the spirit and physical world was weakest on this night, allowing evil spirits to roam the earth. Druids believed that if the spirits weren't provided with food, shelter and entertainment, they would cast spells on the living and destroy their homes.[19]

In an attempt to appease the evil spirits, the Druids would light bonfires. Revelers would dance around the fire and run through the flames to entertain the spirits. Often, these ceremonies included human sacrifices. The custom of wearing costumes sprang from an attempt by the people to disguise themselves from any evil spirits who may have been looking for them.[20]

As St. Patrick brought the message of Christ to the Celtic people, he worked to do away with these pagan practices by helping to establish All Saint's Day on November 1. Pope Gregory IV made the holiday official in AD 900. Thus, October 31 became known as "all Hallows' eve"—or "Halloween."[21]

In 1517, Martin Luther, who is credited with sparking the Reformation movement, chose October 31 to nail his ninety-five theses outlining abuses of the Roman Catholic Church on the door of Castle Church in Wittenberg, Germany. Luther chose this date because he knew that people would be attending mass the next morning. As a result, October 31 is also known as Reformation Day to many Christians.[22]

Halloween was not widely celebrated in the United States until the late 1800s when many Irish people began to immigrate to the United States.[23] By the mid-1900s, Halloween had become chiefly a holiday for children. Adult interest in Halloween began to surge once again in the 1970s with costume parties, etc. Today, the money spent on Halloween decorations, candy and costumes ranks second only to Christmas sales.[24]

Although Halloween seems to masquerade as all fun and games, it is still observed as Samhain for the Wicca religion and is celebrated throughout the United States. In fact, many practicing witches and pagans continue to consider October 31 as their highest holy day.[25]

A Closer Look

"Everything is permissible"—but not everything is beneficial. (1 Corinthians 10:23)

Fall may be my favorite season, but I really dread Halloween. To me, Halloween is about witchcraft, paganism and the occult, and I'd prefer to just ignore the holiday altogether. But to children, mine included, Halloween is about one thing: *candy*. The goal of every child is to collect as much candy as humanly possible on Halloween night so he has a "stash" that might last until Christmas!

With costumed children on our doorsteps salivating for Snickers and jack-o-lanterns lighting up the streets, what should Christian parents do about Halloween? That's a very good question, and one without an easy answer.

The Bible is very clear about steering clear of sorcery, witches and demons, but does that mean that we should shut our doors to trick-or-treaters? Or refuse to allow our children to dress up as princesses and cowboys and collect their weight in candy? How about participating in church-sponsored Halloween alternatives? But aren't these types of activities simply bowing to the culture? Again, hard questions with no easy answers. This is why I dread Halloween!

We basically have three choices when it comes to Halloween:

- Decide not to participate in any Halloween activities. Perhaps go out to dinner and a movie to avoid trick-or-treaters.
- Participate in a church-sponsored Halloween alternative or plan a party of your own.
- View the custom of trick-or-treating as an opportunity to share the love of Jesus. Perhaps include a tract or Bible verse with the treats you hand out, or set up a "rest stop" for weary parents in your driveway by putting out some lawn chairs and offering hot cider.[26]

The bottom line is that the "Halloween question" is between you and God, and it's one that shouldn't be taken lightly. Spend some time in prayer and in reading your Bible and ask God to guide you regarding His will for you and your family.

Do not be overcome by evil, but overcome evil with good. (Romans 12:21)

Table Talk

- Why do you think Halloween is such a popular holiday?
- Do you think trick-or-treating is wrong? Why or why not?
- Do you think Christians should participate in any Halloween activities? Why or why not?
- What could a family choose to do instead of participating in Halloween?
- What can you do to reach out with the love of Jesus to the neighbors who come to your home on Halloween?

Celebrate!

Preschool and Above

- Attend a Halloween alternative sponsored by a local church or other Christian group. Or get together with your friends and host one of your own.

Elementary Age and Above

- Host a "Heroes of the Faith" party. Ask kids to come dressed as their favorite Bible character, missionary or other Christian they admire. Be sure to plan a time when partygoers can explain what made them choose their costumes.

Teens and Above

- Spread the love of Jesus by setting up a parent "rest stop" in your driveway on Halloween night. Set out lawn chairs and serve hot cider.

Recipes to Enjoy

Here are a few of our favorite fall recipes to warm up your family!

Cyndy's Chili

This chili swept the awards at my daughter's youth group chili cook-off, racking up trophies for everything from "Best Recipe" to "True Belly Bomber." I must warn you, however, that I don't think a pot of chili is worth beans if it doesn't make you sweat!

1 1/2 pounds ground beef
1 t. chopped garlic
1 large onion, chopped
1 large green pepper, chopped
1 packet of chili seasoning mix
3 16-ounce cans chopped tomatoes
4 16-ounce cans dark red kidney beans

1 15-ounce can tomato sauce
1 cup water
1 1/4 t. coarse black pepper
3/4 t. chili powder
1 1/2 t. ground cumin
1 t. salt
2 T. sugar
1/4-1/2 t. red pepper (according to taste)

Brown the ground meat with the onion, garlic and green pepper. Remove the excess fat and stir in the seasonings. Add the rest of ingredients and let simmer for at least one hour, stirring frequently. Makes 12 cups.

Crispy Pumpkin Treats

6 cups crispy rice cereal
1 bag mini marshmallows
1/4 cup butter or margarine
Yellow and red food coloring
Green gum drops

Melt butter and marshmallows over low heat in a large pot. Tint the mixture with food coloring to make an orange color. Stir in the cereal. With buttered hands, shape the mixture into pumpkins. Add gumdrops to top before the mixture cools. Cool completely on waxed paper. Enjoy!

Spiced Apple Cider

1 gallon apple juice or cider
1 T. whole spices (allspice, cinnamon sticks, cloves)
1 orange, sliced (optional)
1/4 cup brown sugar

Heat apple juice or cider to boiling. Add spices (tied in a cheesecloth or in a tea ball) and steep on low heat for 30 minutes. Remove the spices and stir in the sugar. Float orange slices on top, if desired.

Notes

1. Charles Crismier, *Renewing the Soul of America* (Richmond, VA: Elijah Books, 2002), p. 58.
2. Timothy Crater and Ranelda Hunsicker, *In God We Trust: Stories of Faith in American History* (Colorado Springs, CO: Cook Communications, 1997), p. 19.
3. Lucille Recht Penner, *Celebration: The Story of American Holidays* (New York: Macmillan, 1993), pp. 12-3.
4. Samuel Elliot Morrison, "Christopher Columbus," *The World Book Encyclopedia Volume 4* (Chicago, IL: Field Enterprises Educational Corporation, 1969), p. 692.
5. Ibid, p. 692.
6. Crater, p. 19.
7. Ibid.

8. Morrison, p. 693.
9. Peter Marshall and David Manuel, *The Light and the Glory* (Grand Rapids, MI: Baker Book House, 1977), p. 41
10. United States Embassy, "Columbus Day" [on-line], November 11, 2002. Available from: <http://www.usembassy.de/usa/holidays-columbus.htm>.
11. Ibid.
12. Ibid.
13. Ibid.
14. Ibid.
15. "Columbus Day" [on-line], May 17, 2004. Available from: <http://chiff.com/home_life/holiday/columbus.htm>.
16. Marshall and Manuel, p. 17.
17. Kim Roberts, "Skeletons in Christianity's Closet," *Omaha World Herald*, Omaha, NE, October 26, 2002, pp. E1-2.
18. Wilson Walls, "Druidism," *The World Book Encyclopedia, Volume 5* (Chicago, IL: Field Enterprises Educational Corporation, 1969), p. 289.
19. Steve Russo, *Halloween: What's a Christian to Do?* (Eugene, OR: Harvest House, 1998), pp. 9-10.
20. Ibid., pp. 10-1.
21. Ibid., p. 11.
22. George L. Mosse, "Reformation Day," *The World Book Encyclopedia, Volume 12* (Chicago, IL: Field Enterprises Educational Corporation, 1969), p. 458.
23. Roberts, p. E2.
24. Russo, p. 13.
25. Mike Nichols, "All Hallow's Eve" [on-line], October 8, 2002. November 12, 2002. Available from: <http://www.geocities.com/Athens/Forum/7280/samhain.html>.
26. Russo, pp. 90-1.

November

Hebrew: **Bul** (see 1 Kings 6:38)

Veterans Day
November 11

Thanksgiving Day
Last Thursday in November

There was joy and gladness . . . feasting and **celebrating***. (Esther 8:17)*

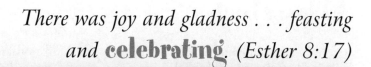

Veterans Day
November 11

Key Verse

I thank my God every time I remember you. (Philippians 1:3)

A Little History

It was the eleventh hour of the eleventh day in the eleventh month of 1918 when the world celebrated as a treaty was signed, officially ending what was known as "the war to end all wars": World War I. One year later, on what came to be known as Armistice Day, Americans came together to remember and honor the sacrifices of the men and women who served during the war. Soldiers who survived the war marched in parades and were honored by speeches and ceremonies recognizing their contributions to peace throughout the world.

Congress declared Armistice Day a national holiday in 1938. By that time, there was unrest in much of the world, and Americans realized that World War I would not be the last war. After World War II, which was even bloodier than the first, Armistice Day continued to be observed. In 1954 Congress changed the name of the holiday to Veterans Day in order to include veterans of all United States wars.

Today, Americans honor the service and sacrifice of our armed forces in the past as well as the present on Veterans Day. An official national ceremony takes place at Arlington National Cemetery at the Tomb of the Unknown Soldier (also called the Tomb of the Unknowns). A combined color guard, representing all the branches of the military, executes "Present Arms" at the tomb, a presidential wreath is placed on the graves and a bugler plays "Taps." In communities across the county, there are parades, ceremonies and speeches. At 11 o'clock in the morning, Americans are encouraged to observe a moment of silence to remember those who fought for freedom.

A Closer Look

Is life so dear, or peace so sweet, as to be purchased at the price of chains and slavery? Forbid it, Almighty God! I know not what course others may take; but as for me, give me liberty or give me death!

—Patrick Henry, March 23, 1775[1]

I'll be honest with you—it is quite uncomfortable for me to take "a closer look" at Veterans Day. I am ashamed to admit that it wasn't until recently that I began to understand and appreciate the great freedom we enjoy as citizens of the United States. I am even more ashamed to admit that I had little appreciation for its cost.

I grew up in an era when military service was not valued by a very vocal segment of our nation, much less honored. As a child, I witnessed night after night of students and others protesting the controversial Vietnam War on the evening news. Veterans who had put their lives on the line in service to their country were not welcomed home as heroes, but as outcasts. It was a time when I found it hard to imagine why anyone would voluntarily choose to enter the military. Looking back, the only word for our nation's treatment of our veterans during that period is *appalling*.

It wasn't until the terrorist attacks of September 11, 2001, that I began to peek outside of my comfortable cocoon in the United States at life in countries with little freedom. I saw the cruel treatment of women in many Middle Eastern countries as they were beaten for appearing on the street without male escorts—even if their only reason for venturing out was to purchase food for their children. I saw how girls in these countries are denied access to education and have no choice in their marriage partners. I learned of people—even children—in Sudan who are tortured and murdered because they refuse to deny their faith in Jesus. In China, pregnant women are forced to abort their unborn children to comply with laws on family size. In Central American countries, those who publicly disagree with governmental policies often "mysteriously" disappear, never to be seen again. The list of human rights violations and atrocities outside of the United States is extensive.

And here I sit, in the wealthiest nation on earth, free to attend the church of my choice, to own as many Bibles as I can afford, to choose my own husband (or choose not to marry) and to vote for the leaders of my government. And why can I enjoy these freedoms? Because the men and women in our armed forces understand that freedom has a cost. And since the birth of our nation, brave men and women have stepped forward, weighed the cost and chosen to lay down their lives in service to their fellow countrymen. Saying, "Thank you," just isn't enough. We need to pass these truths on to future generations—and Veterans Day is a great place to start.

Greater love has no one than this, that he lay down his life for his friends. (John 15:13)

Table Talk!

- What does freedom mean to you?
- What are some examples of freedoms that we enjoy in the United States but that may not be available to people in other countries?
- What do you think motivates a person to join the armed forces?
- What can we do to show appreciation to those who serve in the military?
- Jesus came to set us free (see Galatians 5:1). Free from what? How was this freedom achieved? Do you see any correlation between the freedom we receive through Jesus Christ and the choices people make to serve in the military?

Celebrate!

Preschool and Above

- Make a card and deliver it to a person serving in the military.
- Invite the child of a military family over to play.

Elementary Age and Above

- Prepare a treat and deliver it to a veterans' hospital.
- Adopt a serviceman or woman serving overseas as a pen pal. Send a care package and/ or regular letters or e-mails. You can find out more information about corresponding with a person serving overseas by contacting the family support center at a military base or visit the military moms Web site at: http://www.militarymoms.net/sot.html.

Teens and Above

- Offer to cut the lawn, shovel snow or baby-sit as a favor to a military family who has a member serving overseas.
- "Adopt" a veteran to visit at a local veterans' hospital or nursing home.

Recipes to Enjoy

Chipped Dried Beef on Toast

This recipe, adapted from 1942 The Army Cook, *was often served in military chow lines during both World War I and II. It was also the subject of many jokes about the sad state of food in the armed services. What does your family think?*

> 2 packages chipped or sliced dried beef
> 2 T. butter or margarine
> 3 T. flour
> 1/2 cup evaporated milk
> 1 cup beef broth
> 1 t. parsley
> Salt and pepper to taste
> 8 slices toast

Melt the butter in a large skillet and add the flour. Cook for a few minutes until the flour and butter mixture browns slightly. Add the milk and beef broth, stirring constantly to prevent lumping. Add the dried beef and cook for 5 minutes. Add the parsley, salt and pepper. Serve hot on toast.

Old Glory Cake

Show your patriotism with this red, white and blue treat!

1 package white cake mix
Red and blue liquid food coloring
1 8-ounce container whipped topping, thawed
Red, white and blue candy sprinkles

Prepare cake mix according to package directions. Put batter in two 8- or 9-inch round cake pans. Swirl one pan with one drop of red food coloring. Do the same with blue in the other pan. Bake as directed. Cool completely.

Remove cakes from pans. Spread the top of one cake with whipped topping. Place the second cake on top and frost entire cake with whipped topping. Decorate cake with candy sprinkles.

Patriotic Fruit Salad

Toss together red, white and blue fruit such as: red grapes, sliced strawberries, raspberries, cherries, blueberries, blackberries, cubed watermelon, sliced bananas, etc. Serve in white or clear bowl and garnish with a small flag, if desired.

Thanksgiving Day
Last Thursday in November

Key Verse

Give thanks to the LORD, for he is good. (Psalm 136:1)

A Little History

Having undertaken, for the glory of God and advancement of the Christian faith and honor of our King and country, a voyage to plant the first colony in northern parts of Virginia, do these present solemnly and mutually in the presence of God and one another, covenant and combine ourselves together into a civil body politic.

—Mayflower Compact, November 11, 1620[2]

Most Americans are very familiar with the story of the Pilgrims who, after surviving a dangerous transatlantic voyage and a winter rife with sickness and starvation, celebrated the first Thanksgiving with their new Native American friends. But this is just part of the story. There are many details about the origins of this important holiday that are often left out of the history books. For example:

- The original band of Pilgrims actually began their voyage from Holland. The Pilgrims were English citizens who were forced to leave their homes in England to escape religious persecution. The group, called "Separatists," disagreed with the Church of England, which placed the reigning king or queen at the head of the Church. The Separatists firmly believed that only Jesus Christ could be acknowledged as head of the Church. They chose to "separate" from the Church of England and worship independently. As a result, they were ridiculed, spied upon, thrown into prison and forced to pay assessments to the Church of England. To escape this persecution, the Separatists sought asylum in Holland. They stayed in Holland for more than a decade and then decided to begin a colony in America.[3]
- The Pilgrims began their transatlantic voyage on two ships: the *Mayflower* and the *Speedwell*. After having to turn back several times due to problems with the *Speedwell*, the Pilgrims decided to abandon the ship and crowd onto the *Mayflower*.[4] These brave Christians crossed the Atlantic Ocean with 102 people crowded into a space about the size of a volleyball court.[5]
- During the tumultuous voyage, the Pilgrims were taunted by the crew. One sailor even called them a bunch of "psalm-singing puke-stockings" and predicted their imminent demise. He even said he looked forward to tossing their bodies overboard.

It's ironic that this same sailor contracted a mysterious disease during the voyage and died. From that point on, the crew refrained from taunting the weary Pilgrims.[6]

- The Pilgrims didn't plan to settle at Plymouth. The settlers actually wanted to establish their colony in northern Virginia. However, conditions at sea made it impossible for them to land at their intended site. Thankfully, what appeared to be a calamity turned out to be a blessing. Plymouth provided the colony with a gently sloping building site with excellent drainage and four spring-fed creeks nearby, as well as a twenty-acre site (abandoned several years earlier) which was cleared and ready to plant.[7]

- Almost half of the Pilgrims died from starvation and disease the first winter at Plymouth. Their bodies were weakened by their long voyage, and the work of establishing the colony was demanding. As a result of these factors, the Pilgrims succumbed to a variety of illnesses, losing 47 of their original 102 members before spring arrived. In the midst of their sorrow, however, the colonists demonstrated the love of Christ by caring for the sailors who had taunted them on the voyage. William Bradford writes,

> A proud young man who would often scoff and curse at passengers confessed that he did not deserve [their care]; he said he had abused them in word and deed. "Oh!" said he, "you, now I see, show your love like Christians indeed to one another, but we let one another lie and die like dogs."[8]

- The Pilgrims learned how to farm, fish and hunt in the New World with the help of an Indian who spoke English and was a Christian. Squanto, a member of the Pawtuxet tribe, was kidnapped as a young man and taken to England where he learned English and became a Christian. He helped the Pilgrims make friends with nearby Indian tribes and also taught them to grow corn, hunt deer and catch fish. Squanto even taught the Pilgrims how to use fish as a fertilizer to help increase their harvest.[9] William Bradford writes, "Squanto continued with them and was their interpreter and was a special instrument sent of God for their good beyond their expectation."[10]

- Ninety extra guests showed up for the first Thanksgiving dinner. The Pilgrims had invited the chief of a nearby Indian tribe and a few others to join them for dinner after their harvest. Little did they know that the chief would show up with ninety braves. The Pilgrims graciously welcomed their guests. This may be why the first Thanksgiving dinner lasted three days![11]

- The harvest of 1621 did not mark the end of the Pilgrims' food shortage. Due to the unexpected arrival of thirty-five more colonists—who turned up without food, clothing or supplies—the Pilgrims had to face the fact that their food supply would not take them into summer. So, even after a bountiful harvest, the colony had to live on a ration of five kernels of corn per day during the winter of 1621-1622.[12] However, even though they faced another season of hardship, the Pilgrims remained faithful and declared a second Thanksgiving in 1622. William Bradford writes, "But these things did not dismay them (though they did sometimes trouble them) for their desires were set on the ways of God, and to enjoy His ordinances; but they rested on His providence and knew Whom they had believed."[13]

After the first two Thanksgivings, there are no records indicating that the day was regularly observed until the time of the American Revolution. The Continental Congress designated several Thanksgiving Days as times to rejoice for victories during the war. In 1789 President George Washington set aside Thursday, November 26, in order to honor the adoption of the United States Constitution, proclaiming,

> It is the duty of nations to acknowledge the providence of Almighty God, to obey His will, to be grateful for His benefits, and humbly to implore His protection and favor.[14]

As the years progressed, there was scattered observance of Thanksgiving across the nation. Soon, a movement was begun to create a national Day of Thanksgiving. One of the chief promoters of this idea was Sarah Josepha Hale, the editor of *Godey's Lady's Book*. For forty years Mrs. Hale wrote editorials calling for the official establishment of the holiday. Her efforts finally paid off when, after the battle of Gettysburg, President Abraham Lincoln declared the last Thursday in November as Thanksgiving Day. Presidents in later years followed Lincoln's example, making Thanksgiving an annual event.

> Thus from the earliest recorded history, Americans have thanked God for their blessings. In our deepest natures, in our very souls, we like all mankind, since the earliest origins of mankind, turn to God in time of happiness. In God we trust.
> —Franklin D. Roosevelt, Thanksgiving Proclamation, 1938[15]

A Closer Look

Mother Goose's Old Wives' Program for Thanksgiving Week

Monday: Wash
Tuesday: Scour
Wednesday: Bake
Thursday: Devour

There are two words that send my normally calm husband into panic as Thanksgiving Day approaches, and they are not *dry turkey* or *lumpy potatoes*. The two words that make him break out in a cold sweat are *Martha Stewart*. My husband knows how easy it is for me to get caught up with preparations in the quest for the perfect, Martha-Stewartesque Thanksgiving that I drive everyone in the house crazy in the process. In fact, there was a time when John would have rather eaten his turkey dinner in a restaurant than suffer through my Thanksgiving "extravaganza."

Yet God calls us to "practice hospitality" (Romans 12:13)—even if we aren't Martha Stewart. As we take a look back at those who were gathered at the table for the first Thanksgiving, we see a powerful example of Christian hospitality. From that first celebration we can draw several principles to help us put the practice of hospitality into the proper perspective and once again open our hearts and homes to others.

Principle #1: Don't get so caught up with preparations that you lose sight of the blessing.

What would you do if ninety extra people showed up at your home for dinner? As you read in the history section, that's exactly what happened to the Pilgrims on the first Thanksgiving. They had invited an Indian chief and a few friends from a nearby tribe to join their celebration, and the chief—obviously thinking "the more the merrier"—brought ninety braves with him!

Just imagine the Pilgrim women's panic as they watched this group descend on the colony. I can hear them now: "Where will we get enough chairs?" "What about dishes?" "Never mind about that, Prudence! How in the world are we going to feed this crowd?"

Granted, the Indians did bring along five deer and a bunch of wild turkeys, but I can just guess who ended up with the job of dressing and cooking them while the men enjoyed the seventeenth century's equivalent to football.

So did the Pilgrims panic? Well, perhaps just a bit. But the bottom line is that they welcomed their guests with open arms, threw a few more pumpkins in the pot and announced that dinner might be a little later than they had anticipated.

We can learn a lot from our industrious forefathers about the practice of hospitality. This year, I'm going to relish the unexpected and trust God to take care of the details. I encourage you to do the same.

Principle #2: A simpler celebration is often more hospitable.

With their first successful harvest, the Pilgrims had the chance to show the "natives" a real English feast. However, instead of simply subjecting their Native American friends to the foods that delighted the English palate, these gracious hosts welcomed the contributions of their guests to the dinner and even ended up sharing recipes. The Pilgrims taught the Indian women how to make pies from the fruit they had dried during the summer months, and the colonists learned how to prepare Indian hoecakes (a small cake made with cornmeal) with maple syrup. Yum!

What does this have to do with us today? (After all, none of your guests have probably even heard of a hoecake!) I think that we all need to take a step back and evaluate our motives for trying to put on a five-course dinner or insisting that the house passes the white-glove test. I know that when I examined my heart and my plans for our Thanksgiving feast, I saw a lot of pride behind my actions. I was much more concerned with people's impressions of my food and my house than I was with how much my guests were enjoying themselves.

Therefore, my advice for you, which I gleaned from the Pilgrims' example, is: Loosen up! If guests offer to bring a dish (or two or three), say, "Yes!" And skip vacuuming under the sofa (the only one who will notice is the dog).

Principle #3: God usually accomplishes the extraordinary through the ordinary.

The offer of a warm meal or a place to sleep may seem like just a small act of kindness, but God often uses a simple gift of hospitality to reap blessings for years to come. This is no more clearly illustrated than in a story told to me by my friend Floy.

> My great-grandparents, who were homesteaders in Nebraska during the late 1800s, encountered a snowstorm as they were traveling to Nebraska by covered wagon from their home in eastern Iowa. Near evening they sought shelter in a grove of trees. A nearby settler noticed them and welcomed them into his home. The next evening, as they reached the site of their new homestead, a neighbor welcomed them into his home with warm hospitality. The generous hospitality of these people impressed my great-grandparents so much that they vowed that they would be quick to help anyone in need.
>
> Their opportunity came about six months later when my great-grandmother woke up on a cold morning to the sound of a baby crying. When my great-grandfather investigated, he found an Indian family who had taken shelter not far from the house. My great-grandmother quickly made up a big pot of cornmeal mush and invited the family indoors. The family declined the invitation, so my great-grandfather helped them build a fire and gave them the food my great-grandmother had prepared, as well as other staples to sustain them as they continued on their way.
>
> This simple act of hospitality deeply touched the young Indian family. For many years, the family left an Indian pony tied to my great-grandfather's fence each year as an expression of gratitude.

What a beautiful example of the blessings of hospitality!

Principle #4: Use your home to bring glory to God, not yourself.

The Pilgrims were extremely humble people who were grateful to God for all they had—and even for what they didn't have. With this in mind, I have a challenge for you: As you open the door to your home this Thanksgiving, don't worry if your guests won't smell the aroma of a perfectly roasted bird or notice your beautifully decorated home with not a cobweb in sight or be greeted by your well-scrubbed, impeccably mannered children. This year, pray with me that our guests will instead see in our clear eyes (and relaxed smiles) the beautiful, tender love of Jesus Christ!

Table Talk

- What does it mean to be grateful?
- What are you grateful for this year? What can you do to demonstrate your gratitude?
- Share how you celebrated Thanksgiving as a child or share a favorite Thanksgiving memory.
- How have you been blessed by other people's hospitality?
- What are some things we can do as individuals and as a family to obey God's command in Romans 12:13 to "practice hospitality"?

Celebrate!

Preschool and Above

- Make this fun Thanksgiving treat to use as place markers or just to munch! You'll need:
  - Vanilla wafers
  - Chocolate frosting
  - Chocolate malt balls
  - Chocolate-covered raisins or peanuts
  - Chocolate kisses
  - Candy corn
  - Red gel frosting

  To make a turkey: Use a vanilla wafer for the base. Dab some of the frosting on the wafer to attach the chocolate malt ball as the turkey's body. Use frosting to attach a chocolate-covered raisin as the turkey's head. Use frosting to attach a chocolate kiss placed sideways for the tail. Use frosting to attach candy corn as tail feathers. Use the red gel frosting to make the turkey's waddle. Note: It's probably a good idea to make these treats on a cookie sheet or a tray of some sort so that once the turkeys have been assembled you can put the whole tray in the refrigerator to give the frosting time to harden (at least 20 minutes).
- Moms may want to borrow my friend Kim's tradition of serving only a bowl of plain, cooked, white rice for dinner the evening before Thanksgiving. Explain to your family that in many parts of the world, a bowl of rice may be the only food people have to eat. Encourage your family to pray for people in other parts of the world who are not as privileged as those of us who live in the United States.

Elementary Age and Above

- Make a blessing tree. Set up a small Christmas tree and ask family members and guests to decorate it with items that represent things for which they are thankful.
- Gather some stones and write the names of your guests on them to use as "Plymouth Rock" place markers.
- Use fall leaves to decorate the table. First, dip an assortment of colorful fall leaves in warm, soapy water and then allow them to dry. Once they are dry, carefully press the leaves between the pages of a heavy book for a couple of days. Then make place cards by writing the name of each guest on a leaf with a gold marker. Roll napkins up and tie them with raffia; then slip in a cinnamon stick and fall leaf. Also scatter leaves on the tablecloth as a pretty background for your table setting.
- My friend Allison gives Thanksgiving guests a permanent marker and asks them to record blessings on her special Thanksgiving tablecloth each year.

Teens and Above

- Invite an international student from your church or nearby university to join your family for Thanksgiving dinner. Be sure to share the history and purpose of the holiday with the student. You may also want to ask the student if there is a practice similar to Thanksgiving in his or her culture.
- Place five kernels of corn on each person's plate. Explain that the Pilgrims had to get through the winter on a daily ration of just five kernels of corn. Or, better yet, read aloud the poem "Five Kernels of Corn" by Hezekiah Butterworth (available on-line at: www.worldzone.net/health/landmark/pilgrim.html). Pass a basket around the table and ask each person to name something he or she is grateful to God for as he or she places each of the five corn kernels in the basket. Ask someone to record these blessings in a Thanksgiving journal.
- Make some treats and deliver them to a nearby fire station or to someone else who has to work on Thanksgiving.
- My friend Becki uses Thanksgiving as a time to take a family photo. It's fun to see how relatives change through the years!

Recipes to Enjoy

Quick Thanksgiving Tips

- I always double all of our favorite Thanksgiving recipes such as stuffing, vegetable casseroles, cranberry relish and pies. I freeze half, before baking, in zippered freezer bags. This makes putting Christmas dinner together a snap! To ensure quality, freeze food flat in the bags, making sure all the air is removed.
- My friend Rosemary bakes her stuffing in a ring mold so she can put her dish of cranberry relish in the center when serving.
- Keep mashed potatoes warm in a slow cooker set on low.
- For a new twist on mashed potatoes, throw two or three cloves of peeled garlic into the water as you boil the potatoes and then mash them as usual.

Janet's Stuffing

I received this simple and delicious recipe from my hairstylist when I was stressing out about preparing my first Thanksgiving dinner. It has been a family favorite for almost twenty years!

One loaf white bread
4 stalks of celery, sliced (you could also dice it, but I like to see the nice pieces of green celery in the stuffing)
1 large onion, chopped
1/2 cup butter

3 eggs
1/2 t. poultry seasoning
Chicken broth (about 1 cup)
Salt and pepper to taste

Toast the bread lightly in a toaster and then tear each slice into 6-7 pieces. (My kids have always loved to do this!) Sauté the onion and celery in butter until soft. Pour over bread. Add seasoning and eggs. Mix well (I use my hands). Slowly add the chicken broth until the stuffing reaches the level of moistness you like. Season with salt and pepper. Stuff the turkey cavities (don't pack them too tightly) and bake the stuffing in the turkey. Make sure the stuffing is hot throughout before serving. Or you could bake the stuffing separately at 350°F for about 30 minutes in an 8 x 8-inch pan until hot throughout.

Audrey's Crunchy Sweet Potatoes

Our family didn't like sweet potatoes until we tasted these from my friend Audrey!

1 40-ounce can sweet potatoes, drained
1 t. salt
1/2 cup butter
4 eggs
1 1/2 t. vanilla
1/2 cup sugar
1/2 t. cinnamon
1/2 t. nutmeg

Topping
1/4 cup butter, melted
1/3 cup brown sugar
3 T. flour
1/2 cup chopped pecans

Mix casserole ingredients with mixer until smooth. Pour into a greased 9 x 9-inch baking dish. Mix topping ingredients and spread over casserole. Bake, uncovered, at 350°F for 50-60 minutes. Dish is done when a knife inserted in the center comes out clean.

Cranberry Relish

This recipe freezes very well.

1 bag fresh cranberries
1 apple, cored but unpeeled
1 orange, peeled and cut into bite-sized pieces
1 t. orange zest, grated (zest is the orange part of the peel)
1 cup sugar

Coarsely chop the cranberries and the apple in a food processor. Add the orange pieces, zest and sugar. Let the mixture sit for several hours (at least 2-3) in refrigerator. Stir well before serving.

Notes

1. William Bradford, *Of Plymouth Plantation 1620-1647*, ed., Samuel E. Morison (New York: Alfred E. Knopf, 1952), pp. 75-6.
2. James Dobson, "November Letter," *Family News From Dr. James Dobson*, November 2001, p. 2.
3. Peter Marshall and David Manuel, *The Light and the Glory* (Grand Rapids, MI: Fleming H. Revell, 1977), pp. 115-6.
4. Kate Waters, "Voyage on the Mayflower" [on-line]. September 1, 2003. Available from: <http://teacher.scholastic.com/thanksgiving/mayflower/tour/08.htm>.
5. Marshall, p. 113.
6. Ibid., pp. 123-5.
7. Bradford, p. 78.
8. Elizabeth Payne, *Meet the Pilgrim Fathers* (New York: Random House, 1966), pp. 60-74.
9. Bradford, p. 81
10. Payne, pp. 81-2.
11. Marshall, p. 139.
12. Dobson, p. 3.
13. Bradford, p. 78.
14. "The Evolution of Thanksgiving Day" [on-line], July 14, 1998. May 25, 2004. Available from: <http://www.cbe21.com/subject/english/printer.php?article_id=1990>.
15. "Presidential Thanksgiving Proclamations, 1930-1939 : Herbert Hoover, Franklin D. Roosevelt" [on-line], May 25, 2004. Available from: <http://www.pilgrimhall.org/ThanxProc1930.htm>.

December

Hebrew: **Chisleu** (see Zechariah 7:1, KJV)

Christmas
December 25

And the city . . . held a joyous **celebration**.

(Esther 8:15)

Christmas
December 25

Key Verse

Give thanks to the LORD, for he is good. (Psalm 136:1)

A Little History

The heavens are telling of the glory of God;
And their expanse is declaring the work of His hands. (Psalm 19:1, NASB)

Peace! Joy! Love! Hope! These are the words that well up in the hearts of believers as we celebrate the birth of our dear Lord and Savior each year. But this wasn't always true. In fact, it wasn't until almost 400 years after Jesus was born that Church leaders made a decision to battle the forces of darkness and replace ancient pagan practices with the light of Jesus.

In AD 354, Christians began to celebrate Christmas on December 25.[1] Since the Bible doesn't specify when Christ was born, Church leaders chose this date in an effort to stamp out the pagan winter solstice festival of Saturnalia, or "The Birth of the Unconquerable Sun."[2] Actually, it's more likely that Jesus was born in the fall since shepherds wouldn't be sleeping in the fields on a cold winter night (see Luke 2:8). Church leaders, however, felt that replacing the excesses of the weeklong celebration of Saturnalia with the joyous celebration of Jesus' birth would help new converts give up their familiar pagan traditions.

The decision to place the celebration of Jesus' birth on December 25 turned out to be very wise, for as Christianity spread throughout the western world, the ancient pagan festivals began to disappear. In addition, many of the pagan symbols of the season have been transformed into precious reminders of God's great love for His people that are still used today.

A prime example of transforming a pagan rite into a powerful symbol of God's love is the Christmas tree. In ancient times, the evergreen tree was worshipped by pagans as a symbol of life and fertility.[3] As Christianity spread, believers began to assign new meaning to the tree. Most notable among those trying to change the symbolism of the tree was Martin Luther, who is said to have decorated his family's Christmas tree with candles to represent the stars in the heavens.[4]

Today, the Christmas tree has many meanings for Christians. Ornaments shaped like apples are hung on the tree to represent man's sin in the Garden of Eden as well as to remind us of our own personal sin. It was on a tree (the cross) where Jesus suffered and died to pay the penalty for our sin. But through His sacrifice we have access to eternal life in heaven, which is represented by the evergreen.

It's important for believers to remember that while some of the traditions we associate with Christmas may have roots in paganism, they have been transformed, just as we have by the love of Christ.

For God . . . said, "Let light shine out of darkness." (2 Corinthians 4:6)

A Closer Look

Having a purpose of our own destroys the calm and relaxed pace which should be characteristic of children of God.

—Oswald Chambers

Are you calm and relaxed during the holidays? I doubt many of us would be able to answer that question in the affirmative (if we're being truthful, anyway). Isn't it easy to get caught up in the madness of the season? Just as the Church had to pull people from their pagan practices in ancient times, it seems that the "trappings" of the Christmas season threaten to pull us away from the true meaning of Christmas in today's society.

I am writing this chapter on the weekend after Thanksgiving, the official launch of the Christmas season. Not only are my morning newspapers stuffed with ads, but I also just noticed that the "home" channel is airing six programs in a row on holiday decorating. One show is even titled "Extreme Christmas." What's worse is that I had to drag myself away from the television! (I think I better delete the "food" channel from our program lineup right now.)

Does this strike a familiar chord with you? I find myself getting so caught up in the food, decorating, gifts, etc. that I am in danger of forgetting what we're celebrating. If you find yourself in a similar situation, I have some suggestions that have helped my family replace the stress of the holiday season with the peace God intends us to enjoy as we celebrate His birth.

1. *Seek.* The most practical thing I do to prepare for the holidays each year is take a half-day advent retreat. I get away, lately to the coffee shop near my home, and ask God to shift my focus from my ideas of the "perfect" holiday to how He would like me to celebrate His birthday. I may read my Bible, write in my prayer journal, read a Christmas devotional or just sit quietly and listen. My "retreat" is nothing fancy, just a few hours away from the telephone and my "to-do" list to seek the heart of God.

2. *Simplify.* I think the reason the holidays are so chaotic for many families is because we try to "stuff" more "stuff" into our already overflowing lives. For the past several years, we have made a concerted effort to simplify in the areas of gifts, food, decorations and schedule. For example, we only buy three gifts for each of our children because three gifts were presented to the baby Jesus by the Wise Men. I now gladly admit that refrigerated cookie dough and canned frosting are holiday staples in our kitchen, and my favorite holiday appetizer takes just three minutes to put together.

   In the area of decorations, we have found that less is more. We work hard to keep our decorations simple and pointing to God. For example, a picture of Jesus hangs next to our Christmas tree to remind us of whose birthday we are celebrating. Our mantle is decorated with fresh fruit to keep us thankful to God for providing all we need. We have also come to view "rest" as an activity and make sure that we include plenty of it in our holiday schedules.

3. *Serve.* There are many opportunities to reach out to others during the holidays. The key is to focus on those one or two activities God has prepared for you to do. Listen for the "still, small voice" calling you to open your arms with the love of Jesus.

Each year, God has given our family a clearer vision of how to celebrate the birth of His Son, and from that knowledge has come something unexpected: true Christmas Spirit!

Table Talk

- What do you enjoy most about Christmas? What are some of your favorite Christmas memories?
- What traditions does our family have that help to keep the focus on Jesus during Christmas?
- What can we do to prepare our hearts for Christmas?
- What gift are you giving to Jesus this year?

Celebrate!

Preschool and Above

- Have a birthday party for Jesus. Ask each child to bring a can of food for the needy as a birthday present to Jesus. Share the Christmas story, sing "Happy Birthday" and serve cake or cupcakes from the "Happy Birthday Jesus Cake" recipe found on page 133.
- One of our family's favorite traditions is to venture out each evening during the holiday season for fifteen or twenty minutes to look at Christmas lights. Just load the family in the car, pop in a Christmas tape and enjoy the show!
- Frame some of your children's artwork to use as decorations.
- Make a pretty natural garland by wrapping thin satin ribbons around pinecones and string them on the Christmas tree.
- Reenact the Christmas story with your family. Give everyone a part—even the littlest can be lambs. Use Luke 2:1-20 as narration.

Elementary Age and Above

- Wrap up a gift for Jesus to put under your Christmas tree. Your gift might be an act of service, a donation to a Christian organization or some other kindness.
- Instead of a gingerbread house, use Nativity cookie cutters (found at craft stores) to make a Nativity scene.

- Rent *It's a Wonderful Life* and have a popcorn and movie night with friends and family.
- If you have a real Christmas tree, set it up in the backyard after the holidays as a gift to the birds. Hang pinecones rolled in peanut butter and birdseed and adorn the branches with dryer lint that birds can use to feather their nests.

Teens and Above

- Get together a group for informal caroling in your neighborhood. Participate in the English tradition of bringing along a jug of wassail (hot apple cider) and offering a cup to your neighbors along the way.
- Become a secret friend to an older person who lives alone in your neighborhood. Anonymously leave a small treat and note on the doorstep each day the week before Christmas. On Christmas Eve, reveal your identity with an invitation for the person to join your family at church that evening.
- Make an advent wreath and plan a simple weekly devotional for your family to help you all remember "the reason for the season."
- Prepare some meals for the freezer to make dinnertime easier on Mom during this busy month.
- Make a fragrant centerpiece for the table by hollowing out oranges that have been studded with a few cloves. Slip a votive candle into each orange and arrange on a plate or cake stand around a large candle. Fill in spaces with nuts and cranberries.

Recipes to Enjoy

Happy Birthday Jesus Cake

1 chocolate cake mix
1 can white frosting
Red sugared sprinkles
Evergreen sprigs
One large candle (6" taper)
One small birthday candle for each person at the party

Prepare and bake the cake according to the package instructions in any size pan or in cupcake liners. (You can either make the cake ahead of time or let each child decorate his or her cupcake while you give the explanation.) Frost the cool cake with white frosting. Decorate with the red sprinkles and evergreen sprigs. Put the larger candle on the cake or in a candleholder and light it.

Explain that the dark cake represents our sins. But Jesus paid the penalty for our sin by dying on the cross for us. The white frosting helps us remember that if we believe in Jesus as our Savior, God no longer sees our sins. The evergreen sprigs represent our new life in Jesus. We can now spread the light of Jesus to the world. Have each person light his or her candle from the large candle on the cake.

Cranberry Tea

This is a warm and flavorful tradition at our house.

3 cups fresh cranberries
2 quarts water
2 cups orange juice
Juice of two lemons
4 cinnamon sticks
1 t. whole cloves
3/4 cup sugar

Heat the cranberries in water until they "pop." Turn off the heat. Add the rest of the ingredients to the pot and allow to steep for 30 minutes. Strain and serve warm.

Christmas Salad

This gelatin salad has been one of my holiday favorites since I was a child. My family today loves it just as much as I did!

1 6-ounce package strawberry gelatin
2 cups boiling water
1 10-ounce package frozen strawberries
3 bananas, mashed
1/2 cup chopped pecans
1 cup sour cream

Stir gelatin in boiling water until completely dissolved. Allow to cool. Add strawberries, bananas and pecans. Pour half of the mixture into a 13 x 9-inch glass dish. Allow to set in the refrigerator. Spread with sour cream. Pour remaining gelatin mixture on top. Chill until fully set. Cut into squares to serve.

Cherry Trifle

This is a Christmas dinner dessert my family looks forward to all year long.

1/2 cup sugar
3 T. cornstarch
6 egg yolks
3 cups half and half
2 T. vanilla
1 angel food cake, cut into pieces
1/4 cup apple juice
2 cans cherry pie filling
1/2 cup sliced, toasted almonds

Mix sugar and cornstarch in a saucepan. Mix in egg yolks. Whisk in cream and heat to boiling, stirring constantly until thickened. Stir in vanilla and cool to room temperature.

Sprinkle cake pieces with apple juice. Place 1/3 of the cake pieces in a glass bowl. Spoon 1/3 of the custard over the cake. Spoon on 1/3 of the pie filling and sprinkle with 1/3 of the almonds. Repeat the layers twice. Refrigerate until serving time.

Notes

1. Alan Williams, "The History of Christmas" [on-line], November 30, 2002. Available from: <http://www.christmas-time.com/cp-hist.html>.
2. Lucille Recht Penner, *Celebration: The Story of American Holidays* (New York: Macmillan, 1993), p. 76.
3. Matthew J. Slick, "Christian Apologetics and Research Ministry: Christmas" [on-line], November 30, 2002. Available from: <http://www.carm.org/questions/christmas.htm>.
4. "Christmas Tree Traditions Around the World" [on-line], November 30, 2002. Available from: <http://www.urbanext.uiuc.edu/trees/traditions-world.html>.

You may request information regarding additional resources
as well as Cyndy's workshops and seminars by writing to:

Cyndy Salzmann
c/o Family Haven Ministries
15905 Jones Circle
Omaha, Nebraska 68118

or by visiting
www.realandsimple.com

Other Books by Cyndy Salzmann

Making Your Home a Haven
The Occasional Cook

Notes

Notes

Notes

Notes

Notes

Notes

Notes

Notes

Notes

Notes

Notes

Notes

Notes

Notes

Notes

Notes